Better Than Before
One couple's journey after a tragic accident

ISBN: 979-8-9856847-0-4

Cover Design: Lydy Walker
Interior Layout: Gary L. Jenkins

Printed in the USA

Table of Contents

Introduction

I began writing this book before I knew I was writing a book. I kept copious notes journaling my way through tragedy and much of it is verbatim in this book.

My writing coach kept asking me, "What is the book about? Why are you writing it?"

To get it out. To put it on paper. To put into words something so awful the mind cannot grasp. To purge.

Two reasons I wrote this book: I couldn't not write it. Even if it weren't published, I had to process what happened to my life. Putting it on paper helped. Getting the angst out, the pain, the anger, confusion. It was madness and if I didn't have outlet, several healthy outlets, I could have gone mad.

Having my husband Arthur read it helped. He told me, "I had no idea what you were going through." Understandably, he was focused on himself, his needs, his survival. There was no room for me in his thoughts. Yet the accident happened to both of us. While he was affected physically and emotionally, I was affected too. I lost my husband as I knew him, our life as I knew it. In 2015 Arthur had his accident, my mom was moved from my home into assisted living, all three of my cats died, and I sold my lovely home. So many emotional layers and Arthur was unaware. Only in reading through these pages as I wrote them could he begin to have an understanding of my experience. This didn't happen to him alone.

The second reason is to help others. I was thrust into the medical world with no prior knowledge of how it worked, what questions to ask. I had no idea that he would be released from the hospital so quickly. No idea I would be expected to choose a rehab facility for him. If, through my experience, a family member or caregiver learns something, anything that would help ease their experience, I will have done my job.

Mine is not a lone experience. But most books are written from the point of view of the person experiencing the broken body, the physical and emotional pain. This book is from the point of view of the caregiver, watching someone I love experience the very worst thing I could imagine short of death. Every much as stressful and painful, except it is emotional pain. And we not only support the paraplegic/patient, we must support ourselves.

This is a behind-the-scenes look; my version of events, the experience of Arthur's accident through my eyes. This is my story.

Acknowledgements

This book would not be possible without the love and support of my husband, who held me while I cried through the pages of this book. He held space for me to have all of the feelings while writing each chapter, as I relived each moment over and over again.

I am grateful for the unwavering support of my kids and their spouses throughout the crisis and while writing this book. My children, Kevin, Ashley and Becca, literally and figuratively held me up during the worst moments, and listened as I processed my grief experience through many phone conversations and through my writing.

Thanks to my editor, Kathie Scriven, who gave me much more than editing. Her spirituality guided both of us and she freely shared her wealth of information on publishing.

Gary Lynn Jenkins went above and beyond formatting, working me through tiny details that I missed in the book.

My writing coach, Dorothy Allred Solomon, took me from my first baby steps through my final chapters. She not only helped me become a better writer, she helped me process the emotions that were pouring out onto the page.

Thank you to the many friends and family members who helped me with this book through editing, reading, praying and listening especially Connie, Shelley, Marilyn and brother Al.

A special note and thank you to the many friends who helped both Arthur and me after the accident. The ones who drove to Baltimore to visit Arthur, the ones who helped with estate sales and barn raising and with cleaning the house. And especially Jim, who provided me and my mom with a meal every Wednesday so I would have at least one healthy, home-cooked meal.

For all those who helped in any way, there are too many to mention, but you are all loved and appreciated!

It is through the confidence that my friends and family had in me that I was able to complete this book.

Prologue

We met through a mutual friend when I was fifty and Arthur was sixty-one, thrilled to have found each other late in life. My second marriage, his third.

Saturday, June 12, 2010

From the altar, my new husband and I turn and face the congregation. The minister introduces us, "Mr. and Mrs. Arthur Morton!" A sea of family and friends clap and cheer for us on this nearly one-hundred-degree day. Arthur looks at me, beaming. Then he takes my hand and we begin dancing. He twirls me, in my white dress, down the aisle. I am glowing as only a new bride could be.

We Plan, God Laughs

1

His black suitcase lays open on the unmade bed, partially filled with socks and underwear, shorts and his new bathing suit, waiting to be splashed in the waves. My hot pink Victoria's Secret canvas bag, a Christmas gift from my youngest daughter Becca, is densely packed, waiting in the foyer to be loaded into the car when we leave in the morning for our trip to Chincoteague Island, Virginia. My eighty-three-year-old mother, who moved in with us a year ago, is tucked in bed. It is the eve of our fifth wedding anniversary.

In our bedroom, packing my cosmetics and toiletries, I am as focused as a drill sergeant, lining them up, not wanting to forget anything, when my cell phone rings, startling me out of my concentration. Caller ID shows it's my husband Arthur. He usually calls to tell me he's on his way home and how much he's looking forward to seeing me.

"Hi honey!" I answer brightly.

"Hi honey." Pause. "I've been in an accident." *Stop.* "I think I broke my back." ***STOP.*** It's 9:00 p.m. But it is no time at all because time has stopped.

In those first seconds, I know, on a heart-searing gut-wrenching level, I know it is true. He is speaking the truth.

And it changes everything.

"Oh, noooooo, Arthur, nooooo," I moan into the phone.

No response.

My mind races, searching for another explanation. I've never known anyone who takes care of himself as Arthur does, never known anyone as hyper-vigilant about doctors' appointments as he is. A friend once said, "There are no small deals with Arthur." The sliver of a paper cut may fester and become infected then he'll need to see a doctor and get a shot and antibiotics. It can't be as bad as he's making it sound. Maybe he's catastrophizing again.

"What makes you think you broke your back?"

"I can't feel my legs," he answers.

*This can't be happening. This **can't** be happening.*

I begin to take short, quick breaths, a lack of oxygen in the air, my heart pounding hard. I'm sure Arthur can hear it through the phone.

His words far away, Arthur tells me what happened in bits and pieces.

With difficulty, he had dug his phone out of the left pocket of his pants and called 911. "I couldn't hear the operator through my helmet so I had to take it off." He knew that he wasn't supposed to move, but he had little choice.

An image of Arthur trying to unsnap the chin strap and tug

the helmet over his head runs through my mind. It would be difficult to do lying on his back.

When riding, Arthur, now sixty-seven years old, wore a full helmet with face protection, like an astronaut going into space. On the back of his bike, I wore a halfie, my nod to protection while still enjoying the wind in my face.

I am standing in my living room, staring out the picture window that looks out on the street, not wanting to believe what I am hearing. Arthur lying on his back, looking up at the night sky, unable to move. He must have landed smack on his back, cracking it hard, perhaps on a tree root?

My mind floods with feelings I can't identify; the urge to get to him overwhelms me. I want to teleport myself to him. The reality of getting in the car, driving, trying to find him is too much to comprehend in the race against time, the race to get there before the paramedics, before they take him to the hospital.

"Arthur, where are you?" I want to care for him, cover him and comfort him. I need to see that he is still alive, that he is still okay.

"I'm at the southbound exit where 270 meets 370." I have no idea where that is. Panic is rising in my chest, into my brain, taking up all the space where thoughts should be. How can I get to him?

I hear Arthur's voice move away from the phone, "Can you get me a pillow or blanket for my neck?"

"Who are you talking to???"

Calmly, Arthur tells me, "Someone saw my motorcycle near the guard rail." Later I would learn this man called down the ravine, "Is anyone there? Does anyone need help?"

"Don't let anyone move you!" I say, terrified it would make his injuries worse.

"I have to go;" Arthur tells me, "The guy is trying to find

me." I don't want to stop our connection, I am afraid. Arthur hangs up.

A minute later, Arthur calls me back. "The guy couldn't find me so I used the flashlight on my phone." How did he have the presence of mind to use the flashlight from his phone so this stranger could find him in the dark? I am quite sure in the same situation, I would not be as calm, as composed.

I still need directions. I still believe I can drive over to him. But it's hopeless. I can't get to Arthur before the paramedics do. Instead, I stay on the phone with the stranger, my connection to Arthur, until the paramedics arrive.

"They're taking me to Shock Trauma in Baltimore," Arthur tells me on the phone as the paramedics load him into the ambulance. *What? Shock Trauma? Baltimore?* We have two hospitals less than ten miles away! My mind races to grasp this new information, that the injury is so bad the paramedics decide he needs Shock Trauma hospital which specializes in severe cases. They decline to wait on a Medivac. It will be quicker on the highway, though it's an hour's drive to the hospital.

My breath quickens, my voice is panicky, I'm stuttering, the journey to the hospital temporarily pre-empting the accident.

"How do I get there???" I ask the paramedic whom Arthur handed the phone to. I am on the verge of breaking down, panic rising in my chest. I don't think I can do this. Like a slap, I hear the paramedic say, "The wife is losing it." I quickly hang up the phone.

I need to look up the hospital; I need to find directions. I am powerless to make my mind work, get my fingers to cooperate, make a decision. What do I do? *Oh God, oh God, oh God!* It's the most I can pray.

Do You Ride?

2

*On one of our first dates, Arthur took me to Harpers
Ferry, West Virginia, a lovely historic town with steep
cobbled streets and little shops. We parked on a street filled
with motorcycles, engines roaring, bikers leathered up.
I watched them, longingly.
"Do you ride?" I asked Arthur.
"I did, many years ago," he answered.
"I love riding."
"Well, I guess I'll have to work on getting my license and
getting a bike."
Later, he gave me a greeting card that read, "She dreams
of mermaids and motorcycles and meeting a man who can
dance." I smiled.
"Two out of three isn't bad," he said.*

The beach. We're supposed to go to the beach. He's supposed to come home and finish packing so we can go to the beach in the morning.

I'm falling, falling, falling. I have to get to Baltimore. I have to get to the hospital. Baltimore is a busy city with horns beeping, streets converging and people walking everywhere. What if I get lost and can't find the hospital? Baltimore at night is especially dark, ominous. I imagine drug dealers and crime.

I can't drive to Baltimore! I frantically call my daughter Becca, who lives near Baltimore and knows the city. "Arthur. Accident. Shock Trauma. Baltimore." My voice is high pitched and words are spilling out in incomplete thoughts. She knows me, knows my anxiety about driving and how quickly I need to get to Arthur.

Becca, twenty-seven years old, is a remarkably quick thinker, unlike her mom. "Mom, drive to my house. Derek and I will get you to the hospital." From her house, the drive to Baltimore Shock Trauma is only 15 minutes.

"OK, I can do that," I reply in a child's voice, relieved to have her decide for me, to have a plan, to take over.

10:00 p.m.

In my soft red pajamas, another Victoria's Secret gift from Becca, I look down and realize I have to get dressed to go to the hospital.

I run up the six steps to my bedroom. With its soothing lavender walls, this room that has been my haven for sixteen years. Here, I can breathe calmly and shut the world out. Now I walk in, my mind racing, my eyes unable to focus. Clothes, I need clothes.

Pants. I need a pair of pants. And a shirt. A bra. I definitely need a bra. I find a worn one in the drawer that didn't make the cut for the trip. I take off my pajama bottoms and pull on the comfy pants waiting on the bed for morning and the drive to Chincoteague.

A long night lies ahead. Hospitals are cold. I need to dress comfortably and stay warm. Bra, long sleeve pullover shirt, socks, slip-on shoes.

What else? There's no time to think. I need to think. What do I need to take to the hospital? My handbag, money, my cell phone. I grab a water bottle from the kitchen counter, walk into the living room, then pause in our foyer, cluttered with our red and white cooler, a wicker bag filled with beach towels and sunscreen. My mind kicks in gear.

Charger. I'll take my phone charger. I don't know when I'll be home again. I run upstairs to my bedroom, yank it from the wall and stuff it in my bag. Downstairs again, I grab my keys from the carved wood bowl by the door and head out to the car, locking the door behind me, leaving the safety of my home. Leaving my mother safely tucked in bed.

The Worst Possible Thing

3

Becca's home is always welcoming, with its wide porch wrapped in a wrought iron railing. I only wish I was visiting to play with my grandchildren. Becca phoned both her siblings about the accident. I walk into her home and she hugs me and she tells me, "Kevin is on his way over. Ashley is home with kids while Chris is working."

When Kevin, my oldest, lived with Arthur and me for three years, they formed a bond. Arthur would help him fix his car, walk his dog, help him with his catering business and pitch in as a father would.

Of the three of us, only Kevin is comfortable driving in Baltimore. In the back seat of his little black Cavalier, I find comfort flanked by two of my children, touched they would show up for me. While Kevin drives, Becca pulls up the hospital on her GPS and navigates. Kevin finds the hospital easily, drops us off and parks while Becca and I find the Emergency Room.

My need to be with Arthur is urgent, but a volunteer at the front desk instructs, "Take a seat. We'll call you when your husband is out of testing."

Thirty minutes drag by before I am finally allowed back.

Arthur is covered in white sheets up to his chest, his arms lie at his sides, hooked up to monitors displaying graphs and numbers that are meaningless to me. But he is alive! From that first phone call, I have been in a state of panic, any coherent thoughts obliterated by the thought of my husband lying helpless, unable to walk, unable to move.

I lean over to give him a kiss and affectionately rub his bald head, surprised to see him smiling and making jokes. I expected him to be heavily sedated or in shock or crying, not cracking jokes. Perhaps he IS in shock.

Kevin matches Arthur's mood and affectionately calls him, "Evel Knievel" eliciting a laugh from Arthur. Then, both to keep Arthur's spirits up and out of curiosity, Kevin peppers his step-dad with questions, "Arthur, where did the accident happen? What do you think happened? Did you slip on gravel?"

"I was exiting the ramp where Routes 270 and 370 meet. It's a dangerous stretch of road, filled with potholes and a hairpin turn," Arthur tells us.

"I passed that ramp on my way home from work twenty minutes before the accident!" Kevin interjects, then continues his questions, "Did you hit the brakes hard? Did you lose the bike, overcompensating?"

"Just beyond the overpass, I hit a bump," Arthur tells us, "Suddenly, the front of the bike began to shake while I tried to steer it to the left in the direction of the down ramp. The bike refused to turn, and headed straight toward the guard rail on the right. The handlebars seemed disconnected from the steering column."

It's the last thing Arthur remembers until he found himself down the embankment in a patch of poison ivy. That's when he reached into his pocket for his phone, realized that he couldn't feel his legs, and called 911.

"Oh man! Now mom's never going to let me get a bike!" Kevin says.

"You got that right!" I quip. Not that I have any influence. Kevin is thirty-three years old and married. We attended his Las Vegas wedding in November the previous year.

In the ER, time is a blur as we wait for results from Arthur's x-rays. I pray, "*Please God, let it be a broken leg, a sprained back. Let it not be the worst possible thing we can imagine.*" I am frozen, the experience ethereal. *This can't be happening; this can't be happening.*

Arthur is complaining his stomach hurts. The doctors are concerned about internal bleeding. Kevin tells me, "It's a good sign he can feel his stomach." If he can feel pain in his belly, he has no further nerve damage.

Finally, a young doctor comes in and introduces himself to us. He reminds us of Doogie Houser of TV fame, a twelve-year- old in a doctor's lab coat.

Kevin immediately reads the look on the doctor's face and realizes the severity of the accident. He looks from the doctor to me. I had hoped, I had prayed it wasn't as bad as we thought. "The x-rays show Mr. Morton severed his spine at the T11," the doctor says. *Not a break. Not a sprain.* This is the worst possible news. The impact hits me in my chest, my gut, head butted, unable to breathe. I burst into tears. I can no longer be strong.

I have heard many marriages fall apart following an injury like this. It's easy to see why. I look at my husband and try unsuccessfully to imagine how my life will be now that he is paralyzed. *Oh God, oh God, oh God. No, no, no, no, NO!*

Standing at his side, I look into Arthur's blue eyes through my tears and say, "We'll figure this out together." When Arthur and I were dating, he dubbed us, "The A team!" I remind him of that now, "We're the 'A' team!"

Kevin steps outside to call Arthur's children. Becca asks the doctor, "Will he walk again?" I don't want to have this conversation within hearing distance of Arthur. I believe in the power of suggestion and subliminal messages. I don't want Arthur giving up hope. But the question has been asked.

The doctor tactfully, kindly replies, "We have not seen that happen in these cases."

"What's the next step?" I ask.

"In the morning, we'll fuse his spine and stabilize it."

Stabilize his spine, fuse his spine. Severed. Not just broken but severed. *Severed.* It sounds final. Severe. Irreversible. Once they fuse it, can it grow back together? *Can't they FIX it?*

This is NOT how things are supposed to be. I'm supposed to be home, in bed, with Arthur. Tomorrow is our ANNIVERSARY!

Kevin returns and tells me he was able to reach Arthur's daughters, starting with the oldest, Debbie, who lives in Colorado, then Donna and Diane. He provided the little information he had but tip-toed around the paralysis, wanting to spare their feelings. Instead, he offered a list of things that could have gone wrong and didn't, "He's in good spirits. There's no brain damage, no head trauma." Kevin promises to text them through the night, sending updates. I'm proud of him for how he handled the calls, for being sensitive to their feelings.

Now it's time for me to call Arthur's family. Arthur has twelve siblings. If you want everyone to know what's going on, his sister Marilyn gets the job done. Calling Marilyn also starts the family prayer line.

What do I say? How can I make this call?

"Marilyn? It's Angela." I choke back tears. *Who wants to convey the enormity of an accident like this?* "Arthur's been in an accident. On his motorcycle. He broke his back. We're at the ER."

Next, I call his brother Dr. Pat. Pat can talk to Arthur's doctors and keep an eye on the medical side of things.

Everyone is shocked; of course, they are. Some family members didn't know he rode a motorcycle!

My kids and I stay by Arthur's side while the staff continues monitoring him. I cry and cry and cry. I am not a crier. I don't shed tears easily, but tonight, I cry on my daughter's shoulder, then my son envelopes me in his arms. Tears are a welcomed outlet for the intense pain I am in.

2:00 a.m.

We've been here for several hours. When the surgeon returns, he tells us, "I suggest you go home and get some sleep." I am hesitant to leave, as if by staying, I can prevent further bad things from happening.

"Will you call me if anything happens? Anything changes?" The doctor reassures me they will continue to monitor Arthur. He promises to call me if anything happens.

"You have my cell phone number?" The doctor checks his information. Yes, he has it.

Arthur seems stable, falling in and out of sleep. I reach over the guard rail on the bed and kiss his face, then reluctantly, turn and leave. With Kevin and Becca beside me, we head back to Becca's.

"Mom, you can spend the night at my house," Becca says.

"OK, I'll sleep on the sofa."

3:00 a.m.

When we arrive at my daughter's home, Kevin gives me a kiss and his sister a hug. Should he go back to the hospital to be with Arthur? He has to work in the morning. With his phone dead and no charger, he opts to drive straight home. He tells his wife what happened to Arthur.

Then he goes outside and cries.

Becca goes straight to bed; her children will be up at 6:00 a.m. I lie on the couch and try to rest. I have no peace. There is no peace. There is only shock – did this really happen? There is only pain and fear of the unknown. Fear of the great gaping hole that lies ahead.

4:00 a.m.

My phone rings from the ottoman next to the sofa. Not a good sign. I quickly grab it.

"Hello?"

"Mrs. Morton?" the doctor said, "We've decided to operate on your husband. The pain in his stomach isn't subsiding and we want to go in and make sure there is no internal bleeding or anything we missed."

"Should I come over?"

"Not necessary. We'll call you after the operation."

Should I rush to the hospital? Be there while he is in surgery? I decide it's best if I stay where I am and rest as much as I can. Rushing to the hospital only to sit and wait will not help. Still, sleep is impossible as I try to absorb the enormity of what happened. Arthur is in surgery right now. *What will they find?*

I am so scared. So, so scared. Fear will surely follow me in the days to come, wake me up in the middle of the night and be my companion in the morning hours.

Cancelled Dreams

4

Our fifth wedding anniversary. My phone rings. From my prone position on the sofa, I reach out and grab it off the ottoman. "Hello?"

"Mrs. Morton?" the doctor says, "Fortunately, we didn't find anything in Arthur's stomach area during the surgery."

Thank God! Some relief. I was raised Catholic; I raised my children as Catholic Christians. I have a lot of faith. Yet nothing prepared me for this, this crisis bigger than anything I've had to deal with; bigger than my divorce, bigger than my daughter Becca's open fracture from gymnastics. Bigger than losing my dad. NOTHING prepared me for this.

I look around my daughter's living room from the sofa that

is my makeshift bed. Today Arthur and I are scheduled to drive to Chincoteague with dinner reservations at our special restaurant, AJ.'s on the Creek.

We celebrated our first wedding anniversary at AJ's. When we arrived, the host ushered us to a cozy table in the corner, pulling a red curtain closed as he left, like being on a train in a private compartment in the Wild, Wild West. We sat thigh to thigh, snug in our cocoon, happy and in love. Now, warm tears seep down my face. Wet tissues litter the floor.

6:30 a.m.

From the sofa, I hear feet padding on the stairs. Through my half-closed lids, I watch my daughter walk quietly downstairs holding her six-month old daughter on her hip and her eighteen-month-old son by the hand. I put on a smile for my grandkids and swing my feet onto the floor.

Becca eyes me and says, "Mom, why don't you go upstairs in Q's room? You'll have more privacy and you'll get more rest." I hesitate, then realize she's right. I don't need to be at the hospital until 9:00 a.m., when Arthur will be prepped for surgery. The doctor told us last night Arthur's spinal fusion surgery is scheduled for 10:00 a.m.

I climb the stairs, limbs heavy, and fall into the double bed across from the crib. Q's room is cheerfully decorated in Dr. Seuss; bright blues, true reds, brilliant yellows. The Lorax, Horton and Sneetch dance across the walls.

A few hours rest would be welcomed. I need to sleep. I lay my head on the pillow and order myself to close my eyes. Sleep. I need rest to endure what faces me. I doze and wake up, remembering what today is, what happened and my tears flow fresh. Again and again, I wake up to the horror of this reality. My mind is incapable of understanding that we were not going on a trip today. That today, a day of celebration, has been replaced with a terrible twist of fate, a horrible life-changing accident. I drift through parallel worlds, here in the present with my pain, there on the beach holding hands, digging our toes in the sand, collecting shells scattered along the water's edge. Then crashing back to the cold, sharp reality of hospital rooms, surgeries and cancelled dreams.

I hear voices downstairs. Then my bedroom door opens and my daughter Ashley comes into the room. Ashley, my only child with brown eyes like mine, sandwiched between Kevin and Becca with eyes of blue. She sits on the edge of the bed. I sit up, and fall into her arms, sobbing, soaking her shirt where my head rests on her comforting shoulders. "It's our anniversary! And we're not going to the beach!"

Ashley holds me. She sits on my bed and holds me until I can breathe again.

8:30 a.m.

I glance at my cell phone. It's time to get up and get to the hospital. I wipe my tears and walk down the curved staircase. In the kitchen, coffee is brewing. As I grab a cup of coffee, Dawn, my new daughter-in-law, takes me in her arms. My son and Dawn have been married for eight months.

What a fun wedding it was! A destination wedding in Las Vegas, like a Chevy Chase movie, fulfilling Kevin's wish to have "the tackiest wedding ever!" "Elvis" picked up Kevin and Dawn at the Bellagio in a pink Cadillac Convertible, a crowd of onlookers snapping photos like they were paparazzi. Elvis also performed the wedding ceremony in "The Wedding Chapel" (as if there were ONLY ONE wedding chapel in Vegas,) singing three songs and leading them into their first dance, "Can't help falling in love with you."

Here she is, falling into the family support system as naturally as if she'd been there all along.

Red-headed Karla, a dear friend of the family whom we've known since middle school, joins us in the kitchen. It's like a funeral, everyone showing up.

It is time to go, but I don't want to face what's on the other end. And I have no idea how I am going to get to the hospital, still being afraid of finding it myself. The shock of the accident renders me unable to make simple decisions, numbness filling in the spaces where my functioning brain should be. I am climbing uphill, thick and heavy with burdens of disbelief, overwhelming grief and unbearable pain.

It is decided for me that Becca's husband Derek will lead and I will follow in my car, giving me the flexibility to leave the hospital when I want and not over-burdening Derek with picking me up later.

It's comforting to have your family step up. This is not a given. We never know how people will react, respond or show up when crisis hits. My children and their spouses are doing an admirable job.

Following Derek, I drive to the hospital alone and scared; sad and filled with dread. I drive up to valet parking in front of the hospital. An older man, hunched, approaches my car to take my keys while I sit silently crying. "What's the matter?" he asks kindly.

"My husband had an accident last night!" I cry, gulping air.

In a sweet, gentle voice he says, "It's gonna be all right. Everything is gonna be all right." It's a comfort to hear. I need to hear it; maybe if someone says it will be okay, it really will be.

I stand in line to get a visitor's ID band from the front desk. I walk down the hall and take the elevator up to the Shock Trauma Unit. I am told that before I can see Arthur, I need to check in at the waiting room, where there is a line of people in front of me. I am impatient to see Arthur. I need to see him before the surgery. The staff seems to move slowly, type slowly. Slow motion. Can't they hurry? Or maybe it's my head that's slow, thick like molasses. I am agitated. I pace. I pray, *Please God, help me!* Finally, my turn, "Your husband's name? His birthdate?" They ask me to wait. Again. Urgency kicks in and I worry: *what if they take him to surgery before I get to him? Can't they see how important this is?* I tell them, "My husband has surgery scheduled. I need to see him before surgery."

Finally, they show a moment of human compassion and one of them says, "I'll finish this. Can you take her down the hall?" Relief, however brief.

Through the double doors and down a short hall, I walk to the cubby where my husband is lying in bed, covered in white up to his chin. He appears to be sleeping peacefully. Arthur always sleeps on his back, the death position, hands folded on his chest. Today his hands lay by his sides. Next to the bed are a hard chair and a hospital tray. I lay my handbag and my book down. I touch his arm. "Arthur? I'm here." I expected him to be awake. I lean over the metal side bar and kiss his face. At four feet nine inches, I have to stretch on my toes to reach him. I caress his forehead, his cheeks, run my thumb over his lips.

A nurse comes to check his vitals. I want him to open his eyes, to recognize me. I ask, "Will he wake up?"

The nurse explains, "He's still under light anesthesia from the operation this morning. They didn't want to completely pull him out and have to put him under again." She walks out, other patients to tend to.

I am quietly crying when the nurse returns. "I want to see his eyes. I want him to see me, see that I am here before his operation." It's our anniversary. I want to connect on our fifth anniversary.

She takes pity on me and asks, "Would you like me to bring

him out for a few minutes?"

"Yes! Could you?"

She reduces the medication through the IV drip and says, "It'll take a few minutes, then his eyes should open. I can only give you five minutes."

I watch his face. His eyes twitch, they flutter and then open. Finally, I can look into my husband's eyes, his beautiful blue eyes.

"Hi honey." He turns toward the sound of my voice and looks at me, present, yet not entirely present. "I'm here. I love you." A little smile in return. His lids are heavy, his eyes roll back, his eyes close.

I wipe my tears. I have never cried openly, without worry about who sees me. I don't care. I must look a mess, no makeup, hair uncombed, last night's clothes. I don't care. None of it matters.

Two visitors arrive, ministers from his church. With relief, I hug them both. I am not alone. They ask if they can pray over him. "Oh Yes!" Someone to pray the words that I can't find. The three of us join hands, forming a circle over Arthur, and one of them offers a blessing on Arthur, the surgery and the doctors performing the surgery. Then they both leave. I am left alone again.

I sit on the chair near the bed. A nurse comes in and sits next to me. She says, "Hi. I'm Sue. I'll be in the operating room with your husband." She opens up his chart, begins reading and taking notes. She stops, lifts her head and looks at me. Laying the chart down, she says, "I may know a little about what you're going through.

"My husband had an auto accident and injured his T-11, the same as yours. He's been paralyzed since he was twenty-five. We've been married twenty-five years. I want you to know he can do anything he sets his mind to."

Hope. She is giving me hope. Hope for a future that I cannot imagine. Hope for a life that exists after being paralyzed.

We talk a few more minutes. She says, "I'm gone for two weeks at a time and he is fully self-sufficient. He can man a boat himself; he drives and he flies and we take trips together."

"Can I have your phone number to call later if I have questions?" I write it down in my small notebook and tuck it in my handbag; the number is gold, to be taken out on occasion.

As I sit next to Arthur's bed, waiting for him to be wheeled into the operating room, I reflect on the gift the nurse has given me. What a blessing this nurse showed up, today, at this particular surgery! Someone who could offer me comfort like no one else could. Serendipity? No, it has to be divine intervention giving me hope. Comfort and hope.

Counting the Blessings

5

The doctor bustles into Arthur's curtained room and explains what will happen during the surgery. They will fuse his spine at T_{11}, where it is severed, using a cadaver bone. They keep as much of the undamaged spine as possible, however, they need something to fuse the bone to for the spine to stabilize. I am learning new terminology. The spine is made up of three sections: The Cervical Spine C_1–C_7, The Thoracic Spine T_1–T_{12} and The Lumbar Spine L_1–L_5. Arthur's injury is in the low Thoracic, a blessing since everything above his belly button is functional.

I often tell Arthur what a beautiful back he has. My back is twisted with scoliosis. I am short-waisted and have a rib-hump on my back, a "deformity." His back is long; it's where his height is. In this situation, it's to his advantage.

I ask the doctor how long the surgery will take. "We won't know until we go in; it could be six to seven hours," she says.

When the staff comes to wheel Arthur into the operating room, I walk with him, touch his arm, caress his face, warm tears down my face. I tell him, "I love you," then they turn the corner and continue down the hall. I am lost, alone. And scared.

I take a deep breath. *What to do?* I remain quiet and pray, listen to my intuition, a little nudge. It's time to go home. It will be hours before I get an update on Arthur's spinal fusion operation. There doesn't seem to be any point in hanging around the hospital.

I leave the hospital, offer the valet attendant my ticket; he quickly brings my little silver car around. I plug my address into my cell phone to get out of Baltimore. I have an hour's drive ahead of me.

Around noon, I pull into my driveway, gather my belongings and walk up the path to our porch. Flowers bloom in the front yard. The weather is sunny, warm. The house unchanged. It's a perfect beach day. My husband is in the hospital. He's having spine surgery. It's not a perfect beach day.

I unlock the heavy front door and let myself in. Becca had called her grandmother to tell her what was going on. From her chair by the window, Mom gets up, her face sad as she greets me in the foyer, opening her arms. I fall into them sobbing.

My mother is beautiful. She began going grey at twenty. Now, standing next to each other, we have matching silver hair. It's striking. Like my mother, I often receive compliments. "I want my hair to be like yours!" Both friends and strangers say, "If my hair looked like yours, I'd let it go grey too!"

Mom and I have had a difficult relationship through the years, not for lack of love, which we've always felt, but for lack of her emotional support. Today, she shows up for me, holds me, rubs my back, as I lay my head on her shoulder, grey heads touching.

Mom has dementia, short term memory loss. She can be present in this moment; the next moment she'll forget what you told her. Now she asks, "What happened?"

I relay what Becca told her earlier. Arthur was in a motorcycle accident and is having surgery on his spine. That his spine was severed.

"Will he walk again?" she asks. (It's a question she will repeat every day that I come home from the hospital or from work. "But will he walk again?")

Will he walk again? My husband and I share a deep faith. We believe in miracles. I believe the impossible can happen because I've seen it happen in my life. As my spiritual friend says, "We will not limit God!" by our thinking. Still, the doctors are not hopeful and it's too early to know anything.

I lift my head from her shoulder and step back, holding mom's hands. With a heavy sigh, I realize I need to cancel the reservations for our anniversary weekend. Going to the computer in my office, I find the motel reservation in my email and call to cancel our room. They have a twenty-four-hour cancellation fee, however, when I explain the situation, they decline to charge us and offer, "We're sorry this happened to your husband."

I am tired. Incredibly tired. *How is the operation going?* My mind is thick and slow. Belatedly, I remember I also need to cancel our dinner reservations at AJ.'s. I cannot hold back my tears as I look up the phone number for the restaurant. It needs to be done, it's dreadfully final. We will *not* be celebrating our fifth wedding anniversary tonight at a cozy dinner followed by a walk on the beach, this weekend or ever again.

Should I eat or sleep? Call the hospital? They said they would call me when the operation is finished.

I enter my bedroom, the open suitcase on my bed mocking me. I zip my husband's bag and move it to the floor at the bottom of the bed. Discarded clothes and socks get pushed off the bed onto the top of the suitcase to be dealt with another time.

I change into my soft cotton pj's, crawl into bed and pull the covers over myself. This cannot be happening. This CAN NOT be happening. I sink my head into my pillow, lying on my side as warm tears seep onto my pillow.

Earlier, I texted Arthur's kids and his family about the operation. As word gets out, my cell phone starts to buzz with texts. Debbie wants an update. Donna asks how he is. Diane asks if I need anything. Each time I close my eyes, my phone buzzes. The family wants to know how long the operation is, when he'll be out, will he be able to have visitors. I have no idea. None.

The house is quiet. Mom sits in her corner reading a book and doing her word search puzzles. I alternately rest and pray that God will heal Arthur. I pray for a miracle.

5:00 p.m.

I receive a call from the hospital. Arthur is out of surgery; it went well and he's in recovery.

"How long will he be there?" I ask. "Can I see him?"

"He'll be in recovery for a few hours. They need to clean him up, change the bed coverings." These are things we don't consider, that our loved one doesn't emerge from surgery pristine, ready for visitors.

"When can I see him?"

"He probably won't wake up for a while."

I consider this. *Should I make the hours' drive back to the hospital? Will I be able to connect with him or will he still be under?* For some, it would be a no brainer. Some would race to the hospital quickly to be near him. Some would have stayed at the hospital waiting for the operation to be over. I calculate the time and energy it will take to drive an hour back and forth to Baltimore to see him for a few moments. Should I leave Mom again?

I portion out my energy, living my life as a marathon, not a sprint. I do not have limitless amounts of energy to spare like my mother did. She would remark, "I wish you had my energy!" I am more like my dad, pacing myself, getting things done in a methodical sedate way. My daily decisions are based on my level of energy.

I decide to stay home, take care of myself and call the hospital to talk to him when he wakes up.

When my children call to check in, I wail, "This is not how it's supposed to be. It's my anniversary!" It helps to unleash the agony, the pain of spending this day worrying about my husband, knowing we should be at the beach. *Why aren't we at the beach?* They don't know what to say, how to help. How could they? What could they possibly say?

My phone has been blowing up with texts and calls from Arthur's family. Thankfully, my kids decide for me to take the brunt of calls from our circle of friends. My daughter Ashley tells them, "Call us if you want an update. Mom is overwhelmed."

Later, I call the recovery room and someone holds the phone to Arthur's ear. "Hi honey. I love you!"

He is heavily drugged and responds sleepily, "Hi honey."

"Happy anniversary," I say weakly, not wanting the day to pass without acknowledging it.

"Happy anniversary," he replies. After a short pause, "I'm going to sleep now."

I am grateful to have connected with him, grateful for the woman who held the phone to his ear.

There is nothing else to do tonight except rest. I make sure Mom has dinner. We sit quietly at the round marble table in the breakfast room, a bump-out addition off the kitchen.

How rich I felt when we moved into this home, fifteen years ago! A breakfast room! I'd wanted one since I was a little girl and my friend down the street had one. Others would call this a sunroom. I dubbed it "the breakfast room" the moment we moved in. It has a bay window facing the backyard with a window seat where my plants bloom heartily. Another window faces the neighbors' yard and sliding glass doors lead out to the deck.

Tonight, the world looks drab, our faces joyless as I look around this room I love, sitting at the table my husband brought to our marriage; a gorgeous round marble table top and heavy restaurant-style wrought iron base. It wasn't long ago that I scrubbed that table clean and claimed it as my own. Now my able, capable husband lay in a hospital with a broken back.

Sluggishly, I clear the table and put our dishes in the sink then drag my feet up to my bedroom. Shortly after, Mom stops at my bedroom door, "I'm going to bed, Angela." She tells me every night when she's going to bed. It's sweet. It's her way of connecting.

I open my door; give her a hug and say, "Good night mom. I'll see you in the morning."

While sitting in bed with the TV as company, I receive a text from Arthur with a photo. He's awake and smiling, two of his daughters at his bed. My throat catches. My first thought is, "I wasn't the first one to see him awake!" quickly replaced with, "I'm happy he is awake and smiling and his children are near him." He is grinning from ear to ear.

It's been only twenty-four hours and the blessings from this tragedy can already be counted. The nurse whose husband had the same injury. His daughter Donna by his side. They haven't spoken in a few years. Now, tragedy brings her rushing to her dad's side. Arthur is beaming.

"How is Arthur?" I text his daughters.

"He looks good and is in good spirits," they respond,

I feel a little left out, yet it was my choice to stay home. *Am I bad wife, not wanting to rush back to the hospital? Do I look like an unsupportive wife to his children? Do they wonder why I'm not there?*

It's time to shut down for the night. I brush my teeth, say my prayers. I shut out the light, aware of the empty space next to me, aware of my aloneness on our anniversary. I close my eyes and drift off to sleep, startled occasionally by dreams of Arthur running into the guard rail, flipping over his bike, lying alone and I am not able to get to him. My pillow wet with my tears, I roll over and drift off again.

The Undoing

6

Day 3—Saturday, June 13, 2015

Saturday. I am up early. Well, early for me since I am not an early riser. I pad groggily into the kitchen in my pajamas and slippers. I enjoy these moments of peace and quiet in the morning. My day starts with gobs of coffee and if you happen to be up, please, don't talk to me. I will stare at you and blink.

I've never been a morning person. Growing up, my mother would tease me in the morning, tap, tap, tap me on the shoulder and facetiously say, "Good Morning Angela" until I'd say, "Stop!" Then she would say, "Angela's grumpy!" Well, yes, now I am!

Arthur usually makes our coffee the night before and sets the timer so hot coffee is waiting for me when I come downstairs. Not today. I am reminded that Arthur isn't here to make the coffee. This is no dream.

I drag the coffee can out of the cabinet, fill the receptacle with water. With fingers that feel thick and stubby, I try to separate the paper filters. I miss Arthur. I miss feeling the love of a fresh pot of coffee waiting for me. I stuff the paper filter into the container, add six scoops of coffee. Try to find the button to push to turn the pot on. My brain is not activated until my second cup of coffee. I've been known to add the coffee and forget the water.

Waiting, waiting for the coffee pot to finish. Finally. I fill my cup almost to the brim, add a splash of milk, walk into the living room and sit facing the sun. The air is still, quiet. The hot mug between my hands, needing warmth even in June.

After moving into this home fifteen years ago, I became deeply depressed. For two weeks I walked the floors, sat on the sofa staring and didn't sleep. One snowy night in January I walked out of the house, into the street, letting the cold wet snow saturate my slippers, wanting to feel something, anything except the emotional pain I was in. I feel that way now; wanting to experience anything but this pain.

I normally relish this morning time, suspended between waking up and starting my day. It's a time to connect with God, gather my thoughts for the day. Drink my coffee. Wake up. That's my job. That's my only job. I take small sips; the heat burns the back of my throat, sliding down warming my insides. My mind wanders; I let it. I need a shower. A sip. I need to get to the hospital. Another sip.

When Arthur was here, he would come down the stairs, groggy, eyes half closed, "Good morning sweetheart. Are you ready for more coffee?" Today, I am left to refill my own cup.

I continue my musings. I miss Arthur sitting next to me. We are demonstrative, expressive together. When sitting next to each other, our knees touch. Arthur may take my small hand in his, the hands that remind me of my father's, strong with hairy knuckles. In many ways, Arthur reminds me of my father, who passed away in 1997.

Both skillful men. Anything I asked my dad to do, I expected he could do it. I once gave him a project to make lattice brackets for my porch. He said, "How do you know I can do this?" I looked at him. It never crossed my mind that he couldn't. When my dad visited us, he entered the house with a black suitcase filled with tools, "What needs fixing?" Arthur is like that. Fussing around the house fixing leaky faucets, adding ceiling fans, relentless in his pursuit to keep our vehicles running smoothly.

Arthur has gentle, kind qualities, like my dad, always ready to lend a helping hand. During snowstorms, Arthur spent (I'm not making this up) eight hours shoveling out our driveway, cleaning off our neighbors' cars and shoveling paths for our widowed friends. At sixty-six, he climbed on the roof of his church to fix a leak. He ushered at church services and mentored newcomers in his fellowship.

It is Arthur who could reach my mom. My mom and I have a deeply set history of communication patterns. If I ask her to do something she says, "No, Angela. Leave me alone, Angela." But without our history, Arthur charms her into taking a walk or going for a hearing test. When Mom first moved in with us, she wouldn't go anywhere alone, a hallmark of her existence. She was enrolled in a senior program that picked her up by bus. On the first day, Arthur walked with her to the bus and waited for her to get on, like a kindergartener going to the first day of school.

I finish my coffee and try to meditate. Failing that, I pray, *Oh God, oh God*! I skip my journaling, my mind is too jumpy. I've been keeping a journal since seventh grade, more recently a daily practice rather than the sporadic entries of the past.

Except today. Today I can't afford the time to sit, to be still and focus.

I am suddenly impatient to get to the hospital, eager to see my husband. Anxiety sits in my stomach, curling, worried that Arthur won't be himself. Will we be able to connect today, physically, emotionally?

I quickly eat my oatmeal, jump into shower and get dressed, ready to be out the door by 10:00 a.m. When Mom wakes up, I tell her, "I'm going to the hospital to see Arthur."

"When will you be home?" she asks. It is a repetitive question whenever I leave the house.

I respond kindly, "I don't know, mom." I learned to keep time vague, not to commit a specific time to her. If I am late, she will wait and get anxious.

I close the front door behind me; mom locks it. I feel bad leaving her alone, yet I couldn't possibly take her. Whenever she comes with us, within an hour she wants to go home.

With directions in my GPS, I travel the fifty miles to Baltimore Shock Trauma, again leaving my car with the valet. It's money well spent because I am not quite ready to tackle parking in Baltimore.

I walk through the revolving doors, wait in line at the front desk, ask for Arthur's room and get a wristband. I begin the long trek to the Shock Trauma unit at the opposite end of the hospital.

I have been a robot on "GO" mode, not realizing how tense I am until I walk into Arthur's room. I take a deep breath. *Relief.* I feel relief when I see Arthur. He is dozing and wakes when he hears me. His room is small with several monitors attached to his right arm to check his heart rate, blood pressure, oxygen levels. He's in a hospital gown with pink Styrofoam booties wrapped around his feet. His legs are wrapped from the knee down to avoid blood clots. He breathes in oxygen through tubes attached to his nose, hooked behind his ears. His left arm is mottled dark black and blue with barely any flesh-colored skin showing through.

He smiles. "Hi honey." His voice is hoarse; he is still groggy. I reach for his hand.

"How are you?" It's a silly question. How would he be? He had a horrible accident; he can't feel his legs and he had major surgery. I wait. My eyes on him, wanting the deeper question answered, "How ARE you?"

"Happy to be alive," he says.

"Do you need anything?"

"I'm thirsty." I give him water from a cup with a straw. He hates public water. He won't drink the water served in restaurants. At home we have filtered water; on the road we take water bottles.

"Are you hungry? Have you eaten?" He didn't eat at all yesterday. Food= normal. Eating means internal systems are working properly. If he's up to eating, he's better.

"They brought me food this morning. I'm not very hungry."

I sit with him, hold his hand while he dozes off.

Nurses' assistants empty his bag of urine, check for a bowel movement, change him. We take our bodily functions for granted once we are potty-trained. Arthur's body still does what it is supposed to do; but now he can't sense it or control it anymore.

A doctor comes in to check on Arthur. He says the surgery went well. To stabilize his spine, they fused it in two places on his vertebrae. They added two titanium rods on either side of the spine. The rods limit his range of motion, his ability to twist and bend.

We place a great deal of faith in surgeons. We know little and our options are limited. How far up or down the spine should be fused is a decision made on the operating table. The higher up, the less he can move. Lower is better, however, we don't make these decisions. The surgeon does.

I ask the surgeon, "How long will he be here? What's the next step?"

"Arthur will be here until we are sure he is stable, maybe four or five days. Then he will move to a rehabilitation (rehab) center."

"How long does rehab take?"

"It varies. The hospital will assign a social worker to him. They'll be better able to answer your questions about rehab."

When Arthur's lunch is brought in, I push the tray over to him. I offer him the sandwich, the apple juice with a straw, the fruit cup. He nibbles. I watch as he struggles to grasp the food with one arm hooked up to tubes and the other injured.

Arthur asks me if I've eaten. "No, and I don't want to leave to get lunch."

He pushes his tray over to me, "Here you eat it." I nibble on the salad; food is comfort for me. Some stop eating under stress. I feed my body when I'm stressed, noshing to fill the gnawing emptiness, eating away emotions I can't yet process.

Arthur's cell phone lies next to him in the bed. It will be his lifeline to the outer world during the lonely days and long nights ahead. It will be our way of connecting throughout the days to come, when I can't be at the hospital.

After several hours, it's time to leave. Arthur is resting. I still have matters to attend to at home. I need to check on Mom.

When I arrive home, Mom is sitting in her chair by the window. She asks, "How's Arthur?"

"He's doing okay. I don't think it's sunk in." My eyes are bleary; my bones weary; a nap would be good.

I suddenly remember Arthur had a trip scheduled to Dallas for his fiftieth high school reunion next weekend! Then, he was flying to Colorado to see his daughter Debbie and his two grandchildren! I need to cancel the hotel reservations and cancel his flights.

Earlier, Donna said, "If there's anything I can do to help, let me know." I've learned through the years when people offer to help, take them up on it. I don't have to be a hero and do it all myself. I text her, "Donna, can you help me cancel the reservations your dad made? I almost forgot about them."

"Sure," she texts back. "Let me know the information."

Where do I begin? I sit at the dining room table where Arthur's laptop sits open, waiting for him to return and pay a bill or send an email. Fortunately, he left his email open and I scan to find the flight reservations. Yes, they're here! I give the information to Donna to cancel along with his hotel reservation for Dallas. It's overwhelming and sad. He was looking forward to this trip. He doesn't see Debbie much and the school reunion was intimate, with fewer than a dozen alumni. Everything that was done is being undone.

Back at my computer in my office, I post a quick message on Facebook, "Please pray for Arthur; he's been in a terrible motorcycle accident." A little while later, my childhood best friend, Angel, calls me. "Aaanngelaaa!" she draws out my name with the accent heavy on the first syllable. That one word conveys a lifetime of friendship.

Angel and Angela. She lived down the street from me. We became best friends in fifth grade, inseparable through high school. We did homework together, were cheerleaders together, double dated, attended proms together. We were bridesmaids in each other's weddings. When I go to a class reunion, people still ask me "Where's Angel?" We are "bookmark" friends, the kind you pick up where you left off no matter how long it's been in between conversations.

After briefing her about the accident, she asks, "What can I do? Have you called your boss? Do you want me to call and tell her what happened and let her know you won't be in?" Oh! I momentarily forgot about my job as an insurance agent. Who would have thought to offer that?

"Oh Yes!" I can't face that call. This small task takes a large burden off my shoulders. We agree to keep the details to a minimum, "Arthur was in a bad motorcycle accident. He's severed his spine. Angela won't be in tomorrow or the rest of the week and will be in touch with you."

I ask Angel to spread the word about the accident and to pray for us.

So many people to contact, so many friends from various fellowships. I am overwhelmed, unable to concentrate, nearly shut down. My children know me well. They take over; go through my phone, contact my childhood friends and Marilyn from Mom's Group to get the prayer chain going. We need lots of prayers! Becca becomes the point of contact to keep calls to me at a minimum.

Enlarging the Circle

7

Tuesday, June 16, 2015

Over the next few days, I return to my morning routine, prayer and meditation, lingering over my coffee in the armchair in front of our aqua blue accent wall. I sit facing the bay window. Two hummingbird feeders hang from our porch giving us endless enjoyment watching their tiny wings beat quickly, their long beaks sipping the sugar water. Hummingbirds make me smile. Mom watches them from her chair, fascinated. My daughter Becca has one tattooed on her shoulder.

The first wave of the crisis has passed, the inner circle of family and friends notified. Arthur is on the prayer list for my Moms' Group, a group of spiritual women from my church who have been praying for each other since our children were babies.

Their prayers are powerful. When they pray, it feels like something is being accomplished. There's little else anyone can do.

I slowly enlarge the circle to include other fellowships. I email a couples group we're in, "Did you hear about Arthur's accident?"

"No, what happened?" They don't expect the response to be "He's paralyzed." Accidents happen all the time. A broken arm, a sprained ankle. No one expects to hear a friend was in a life-changing accident. No one wants to hear that someone they care about is paralyzed. It hits too close to home.

No one knows what to say.

A friend who had breast cancer suggested CaringBridge to get the word out. CaringBridge is a website to post updates on a sick or infirmed family member relieving caregivers of the burden of responding to phone calls, texts, emails. We can ask for whatever the patient needs or set up a schedule for visiting. Donna quickly sets up a page on CaringBridge and includes me and Debbie as administrators so we can post updates, add photos or add a task. Later, I discover that Arthur's ex-wife was included as an admin. This would prove problematic.

I visit Arthur daily. Has the enormity of the accident sunk in? As I enter his room one morning, I notice his arms covered with a milky film, red wounds oozing. Poison Ivy. As if the accident weren't dreadful enough, as if a broken spine were not as bad as it could possibly be, poison ivy covers his arms and chest. Oh Arthur! My heart goes out to him. *What can I do to make it better?*

When the hospital phone in Arthur's room rings, he can't reach it. I take the phone from the wall, "Hello."

"Hi Angela, this is Teresse. How's Art doing?" I chat for a minute with Arthur's oldest sibling and hand the phone over to him. Arthur's twelve siblings are spread far and wide. Nevertheless, they do an admirable job of connecting with each other.

Arthur is upbeat, "I believe this is temporary. I see myself walking again," he tells Teresse, me, his friends, anyone who will listen.

In his bed, Arthur's legs are wrapped in special stockings to prevent blood clots and pulmonary embolisms, which he had two years ago following his double knee replacement. His feet are encased in pink Styrofoam pads to keep them straight.

Arthur cannot control his bowels or urine. He pushes the call bell for the nurse's station, "I think I had a bowel movement." It's not an emergency to them. The staff has other patients, medicines to deliver. We wait. Sometimes up to an hour.

Every few hours, he needs to be rolled from his back to his side to fend off bedsores on his bottom and feet. It takes two aides to roll him over. A pull sheet is positioned under his midsection. One aide holds the pull sheet with both hands and tugs, sliding Arthur to one side of the bed where he is gently rolled over on his side by the other aide and held steady with a pillow tucked behind his back.

Arthur has a pump to self-administer strong pain medication as needed. On schedule, a nurse visits and asks, "What is your pain level on a scale of 1-10?"

"About a nine," he replies. Ten is the worst.

The nurse administers additional pain meds, one of which is Oxycodone. Oxycodone is a very addictive opioid drug. Arthur knows too many who have gotten hooked on Oxy drugs following surgery. He doesn't want to stay on the meds longer than he has to; however, the surgery is so recent he can't manage his pain without these strong opiates.

I ask the nurse how his heart rate and blood pressure are, how his incision is doing. His wounds are fresh and need to be checked regularly for infection and seepage. The bandages are changed every few hours. The stitches on his back run the entire length of the incision—about twelve inches long. One long bandage runs down his spine; another covers the incision on his belly. I avoid looking at them. I don't like blood.

A few days after surgery, I am surprised when I walk into Arthur's room and find him upright in a wheelchair. I learned the staff gets patients out of bed quickly. This lowers the risk of pneumonia and other infections that can settle in a prone body

He looks healthy, his color good. He smiles. "Hi, Sweetheart. Good to see you." His smile reminds me of my dad's. My dad never took a bad photo and neither does Arthur. He beams in photos, wrapping his arm around whoever is next to him.

I give him a kiss, ask, "How are you?"

Then his eyes enlarge, his body leans forward. "I'm having hallucinations!" he says intensely, "They are vivid, the colors so vibrant!"

"Are they dreams or are they when you are awake?"

"When I'm awake. It looks like the world is ending! I'm afraid to go to sleep!" He speaks in a hoarse whisper, words bubbling out, terrified of the hallucinations, afraid they are real and afraid that next Tuesday, the world will end. He repeats this to me, to the nurses, to visitors. "It looks real. I can't tell the difference between reality and the visions!"

He calls them day-mares because he has them when he's awake.

He describes them to me, "People were eating and drinking, people were pushing things around, moving the tables, trying to get in their cars as quickly as possible."

"Why?" I ask.

"They were trying to get out of town, find people they loved or find an area that might survive. There was total panic." His eyes are big, his voice penetrating. He sounds petrified.

"Elaborate rooms, like out of Buckingham Palace, books on the shelves, heavy red curtains, heavy leather furniture, big heavy tables. There were people in the rooms. People were racing to find people to be with because people were begging to die, wanting to be run over by cars, they wanted to end it so they wouldn't have to stay around and suffer and wait for the end of the world."

He looks around the room, "Is this reality?" he asks. He explains, "It's like tunnel vision, the line of reality in the center; on either side of the line, hallucination. I try to focus on the small space in the middle that is reality."

Later, he tells me "I was stuck in this delusion with no way to get out. It seemed real because it was clear and detailed."

I don't know what to make of this. Is it the drugs? Is it his way of processing the accident? I later find out hallucinations are a side effect of one of the strong medications he is taking.

A nurse comes in to check on Arthur. She gives him salt pills. "What are these for?" I ask.

"His salt is low," she replies. "We cannot release him until his salt levels are up." Could this contribute to his mental confusion? The staff is limiting his water intake to prevent his salt from being flushed out of his system.

"What is the next step for Arthur? When will he be released? Where will he be released to?" I ask the nurse.

"Patients are assigned a social worker. One will be in contact with you," she tells me. It's Tuesday and we still haven't been contacted by or assigned to a social worker.

Each night I arrive home exhausted to make dinner and spend time with my mom. Each day she asks, "How's Arthur doing? Will he walk again?"

I'm not ready to return to work. Not sure when I'll go back. The details about Arthur's situation are unknown and, emotionally, I'm not ready. I'm not sure I can focus my mind on my customers in the insurance business.

On Wednesday I call my boss to check in. It's a family insurance agency with three of us – father, daughter and me.

I offer sketchy details of Arthur's situation. "He's paralyzed from the waist down. It was a motorcycle accident."

I ask how work is going. "Frankly I'm drowning," she says. My life was just turned upside down and she is complaining to me that she is drowning at work?!

It's not my place to rescue her; however, I like my job and I've been there just six months. I'm worried she'll hire someone else if I don't give her a concrete response. "I want to come back to work," I say. "I plan on it. I just don't know when yet."

I pause, processing. What should I do? Where do my obligations to my husband end and my obligation to work begin? "OK. How about if I come in for a short shift? I can do 10:00 to 2:00 p.m. tomorrow."

I don't know how to fit work in with visits to the hospital and decisions to be made about Arthur's next step. It will be a rehab facility, that's all I know.

With nothing to go on, where do I begin my journey of finding the best rehab for Arthur? It's daunting. It's a huge deal, a big decision. It could be his home for the next six months of his life. A heavy burden of responsibility on my shoulders.

Which Rehab?

8

We still haven't heard from a social worker. Days are slipping by and I am getting concerned, frantic. The social worker is the liaison between the hospital and the rehabilitation facility where Arthur will go for his physical and occupational therapy. I thought social workers were for neglected kids removed from households but, no, they also facilitate patient discharge, transportation and legal authority for release of patients.

When I visit Arthur, I ask "Has the social worker stopped by yet?"

"No, I haven't heard anything," he tells me.

"I have called the social worker department and left messages."

Arthur's rehab is the next step in this journey. The hospital releases patients once they are stabilized with no "medical" reason for keeping them. Sending Arthur to rehab a week after major surgery with his spine still healing and incisions in his stomach and back seems hasty to me, however, that's not how hospitals look at it. Or maybe it's the insurance companies. His heart and blood pressure are within the normal range. He is in no immediate danger. Like patients in a factory, he is pushed out, ready or not.

Before the disaster, Arthur told me, "If anything happens to me, I want Debbie involved in decisions about my care." Although it may be simpler to make decisions myself, it's not a bad idea to bounce them off on someone else. I would want my children involved in decisions about my care. Since these are his wishes, I will honor them and include his oldest daughter. But what if we don't agree? Who gets to make the final call?

The most pressing issue is which facility Arthur will go to for his rehabilitation when he is released from the hospital. I've been told physical therapy is about six months in a rehab with an injury of this kind. Choosing the right facility is critical.

I google "best spinal cord rehabs." A facility in New Jersey. That's not too far. National Rehabilitation Hospital (NRH) in D.C. is suggested by our friend Nancy, a social worker. Craig Hospital in Colorado was highly recommended by Sue, the nurse whose husband is a paraplegic. Her husband spent six months there. Sue told me that in rehab Arthur would learn what he needs to know to be independent–basic needs such as bowel training and transferring as well as how to cook on a stove and how to drive.

I call Debbie to discuss rehab facilities and relay what Sue told me, "Craig Hospital in Colorado is the best rehab facility in the country and known around the world." Debbie and her brother Bob live in Colorado so it's a good possibility. There, Arthur could be near family and receive the best care. My goal is to find him the BEST SPINAL rehab facility, a place with a good record for helping people with spinal injuries. I ask Debbie to look into Craig and, since she lives in Colorado, could she possibly visit it?

Six months is a long time to be away from each other if he does go to Colorado. Another aspect to consider. I have a job here. *Can I give up my job? Should I give up my job?*

It's paramount he learns the skills he needs to succeed as an independent person. I've seen Arthur's determination after his double knee replacement two years ago. He called himself 'The poster child' for grit and determination at the rehab, willing to do the hard work on two knees fresh from surgery.

When he is determined, he will make it happen. For example, I was asked to assist in a service at Arthur's church while he was in rehab after his knee surgery. It was my first time on the altar (in a choir robe that swallowed me whole with its flowing arms and billowy fabric), facing the congregation. Arthur wanted to watch me and he convinced the doctor to let him out of rehab for the night, convinced my son-in-law to drive him to church. Arthur walked up the steep steps of the church, his knees still raw from surgery. As he entered the vestibule I exclaimed, "Arthur! What are you doing here??"

"I wanted to surprise you!"

Arthur is resolute that he will walk again. While I'm hopeful, the doctors have not been encouraging. I'm leaving room for miracles, but today he can't feel his legs or his feet, and he can't walk. He needs to learn how to live life in a wheelchair.

Choosing the right facility is vital. I need to make quick decisions with scant information and little time. Arthur will be released on Friday. Debbie and I narrow it down to NRH in D.C., Craig Hospital in Denver and Kernan in Baltimore. Kernan is recommended by Shock Trauma. It's also the closest and easiest for friends and family to visit.

Thursday. Arthur has been at Shock Trauma Hospital for one week. A week of waiting for the miracle. A week of fear, disbelief and shock. A week of not knowing what's next, of adjusting to this new reality, and of being out of my element.

Before I leave for work, I call Craig to gather information. The answering machine comes on and I leave a message, "My husband has been in an accident. He's paralyzed from the waist down. Can you give me information about the process of getting into Craig?"

How I'm going to fit it all in? Work, visiting Arthur, finding a rehab, taking care of my mom. I show up for work, fill my boss in on the details of the accident and what still needs to be done for Arthur's care. Craig Hospital calls back on my cell phone while I'm at work. This would be the beginning of many calls and conversations during work hours. This is how it all fits in.

"Your husband would need to have an evaluation before we could accept him," someone tells me.

"Does someone come out here to see him?" I ask.

"No, you would have to fly him out here."

"How?"

"You'd hire a medical transport to pick him up from the hospital and fly him to our facility."

How could we possibly afford to fly him out? I doubt Medicare would cover it. What if Craig doesn't accept him?

During lunch, I call Debbie to tell her what I found out. She hasn't gone to see Craig yet. She says, "So, I'm thinking if he's out here in Colorado, his support system is out there in Maryland."

Arthur's support system is critical to his recovery. How would he do without it? Would he be isolated?

We discuss NRH. I tell her, "If he's in D.C., I won't be able visit him as much." I'm afraid of driving in D.C., especially during rush hour. The streets are confusing and people honk at you if you slow down. *Will his friends visit him in D.C.?*

I call Nancy who recommended NRH. "Do you think NRH is a better facility than Kernan?"

"No, I think it's comparable. I'm more familiar with NRH."

I make decisions based on solid research, intuition and a lot of prayer. In a crisis, when my mind won't calm down and I can't hear my intuition, I pray, *Which rehab, God?*

I decide to visit Kernan in Baltimore after work. Kernan is the most convenient and accessible rehab for friends and family. But is it the best facility?

2:00 p.m.

I leave work and call Arthur from my car. "How are you today?" Code for, "Does he have any new issues?" I tell him, "I'm going to Kernan to check it out. I'll visit you when I'm finished."

With trepidation, I plug the address of Kernan into my GPS and begin the hours' drive. I want a sense of the rehab hospital, the rooms, the equipment. Is it clean? How does it smell? Is it well-equipped?

I'm racing against time, bearing the pressure of making the "right" choice, the only opportunity to make this decision. I still don't know who will pay for it, if it will all be paid for or for how long. Because it was a motorcycle accident, there is no medical coverage; however, Arthur does have Medicare. I'll know more when I talk to the social worker. Having many questions and few answers leaves me frazzled.

I'm in Baltimore, anxious about getting lost, tense about making this huge decision and tired from the uncertainties swimming in my head. I pull into the driveway of Kernan, park and walk through the automatic sliding doors without an appointment. I want to see what Kernan is like without someone being prepared for a formal tour.

No one looks up from the front desk. No one stops me, or

asks me whom I'm seeing. Nothing. Mmmmm, no protocol to protect patients from crazy people walking in? I walk over and ask if I need a name tag. The woman points to a basket with visitor tags.

The lobby is large, airy and light-filled. It appears clean and uncluttered. I look for staff – are they engaged or on their cell phones? This won't tell me whether the rehab itself is good; however, it gives me an indication of the level of commitment.

Turning to the right, I walk down a short hallway to a dead end with signs pointing: Right: pool; Arthur would enjoy the opportunity to get into a pool. He used to be a lifeguard and he enjoys swimming. Left: Spinal Rehabilitation. I walk to the left, passing a nurses' station. Again, no one asks if I need help.

The floors are clean with nothing lying about; no dirty tissues or diapers. The hospital doesn't have a nursing home smell, the kind that hits you when you walk in, urine and dirty diapers and old age. As a little girl, I visited my grandmother in a nursing home. I could smell the stench as soon as I walked in the door. A combination of urine, soiled bedsheets and anti-septic, unpleasant reminders that this place is for the dying and infirmed.

I peek in patients' rooms, two beds to a room and not very large. Curtains drawn around the beds offer a small amount of privacy. Most rooms are full of monitors. In one bed a patient's leg is suspended, upheld by a pulley. A young man sits in an electric wheelchair in the hall, his legs silent while nurses and aides walk by.

This facility appears to be clean enough, nothing stands out. *How do I feel about this?* This facility, this decision that was thrown at me because of the accident a short week ago.

Back in my car, I check my cell phone messages. Darn! I missed a call from the social worker while visiting the facility. I frantically call her back and get her answering machine. "Hi.

This is Angela. Please give me a call back as soon as possible."
We haven't talked to a social worker yet and Arthur is being
released tomorrow. Panic is setting in.

Time to visit Arthur. Unfamiliar with this area, I plug in the
address of the hospital and drive away. Driving in Baltimore,
down tiny streets in seedy neighborhoods, I am scared. My
nerves are stretched so thin I can hardly take a deep breath.
My two anxieties, directions and time, are competing for which
is going to defeat me. We have a deadline of tomorrow, when
Arthur is released, to choose a facility. I am doing the footwork,
making the calls, visiting the facility. The rest is up to God.

The phone rings; it's Kim, the social worker. "Hi, I've been
trying to get in touch with someone and no one has called me
back!" I pull into a parking lot in a dingy part of Baltimore
because I can't talk and listen to directions.

She says, "I'm here. I've just been assigned."

Words bubble out, "My husband is being released and we
don't have a facility picked out and I need someone to get transportation and the doctors have to sign the releases." Although
she is calm, I can tell she is put off by my rant. I have to calm
down. I need her on our side. We agree to meet back at the
hospital. I tell her, "I'm on my way."

Arthur is calling. I can't take two calls at once, I'm feeling
overstimulated and this adds to my stress. After I hang up
from the social worker, I call Arthur back. He is distressed,
talking fast, intense.

"I haven't seen the social worker yet! I asked Diane and Melanie to go to the nurse's desk to ask about it." Diane is a young
adult capable of doing this on her own. Melanie is his ex-wife.

"Arthur, I'm on top of this. I spoke to the social worker. You
don't have to involve your ex-wife in your care."

"Well, you weren't working on it!"

"I am too! I've called the department several times and left messages; I visited the rehab facility to check it out for you! I was on the phone with the social worker when you called. Please DO NOT involve your ex-wife in your care."

"You're not working fast enough!"

"I'm doing the best I can!"

"I need to get things done around here!"

I hang up, shaking, angry. Offended he would include his ex-wife. Frustrated that he is not able to appreciate all I am doing. I'm tired of running around, driving in Baltimore, making calls without results. He clearly doesn't remember when I told him about my calls to the social worker.

I have overcome the parking situation and pull into the garage a block away from the hospital. I arrive, my nerves frayed, my shoulders aching, and go directly to Arthur's room, not happy with our last conversation. When I arrive in the room, his daughter and her mother are gone. I'm grateful for that. I cannot deal with them rationally right now.

I glare at him and say hello. He is unsettled and so am I. I tell him, "I talked to the social worker. She called and we're meeting here this afternoon. I also visited Kernan." My heart is beating quickly, "Arthur, I don't appreciate you asking your ex-wife for help. I can take care of you. I'm your wife."

"I wasn't asking her to help with my medical care. I wanted to know about the social worker. You weren't here."

"I was looking at a rehab for you!"

"Diane didn't want to go to the nurse's station by herself so her and her mom went." Diane is a college graduate who has backpacked through Europe and been to the Middle East. Could she really not handle going to the nurse's station herself or is Arthur placating me?

"Arthur, I was on top of it! You're not being patient and you're not talking to me! Ask me before you have someone else do what I'm already doing!"

I hate redundancy. There isn't enough time in the world for redundancy. I don't have the energy to waste on this argument or on doing double work. Having too many people involved can complicate matters. I like simple.

And we've had some boundary issues around his exes.

The morning after the accident, while I was in the room with Arthur waiting for his surgery, a nurse came over and said, "A woman is on the phone who says she is the mother of his children. Can I release information to her?"

It was Arthur's second wife.

With HIPAA, information is carefully guarded and released only with permission. I instinctively felt the need to establish healthy boundaries around who has rights to Arthur's information. My response was immediate and I am adamant. I told the nurse, "No." Arthur's children are old enough to make the call themselves, drive themselves to the hospital. Old enough for us to have direct contact. This, however, would be the beginning of a struggle to keep some semblance of sanity in the midst of insanity, some privacy in a place where precious little is private. It's a battle I would lose.

It hasn't been easy being Arthur's third wife, though his last marriage ended fifteen years ago. He has two children with his first wife, two with his second and a daughter from another relationship.

I came along when a five-year relationship was ending. I didn't want to get involved if he still had feelings for this ex-girlfriend. I didn't want to be a rebound girl. I asked, "Do you need time or space before jumping into another relationship?"

Arthur said, "I thought I loved her at one time but in the end, it was only as a friend."

Friends advised us to "take it slow." We didn't see each other during the week so "rushing" wasn't happening. However, emotionally, we were connected early on, and when we were together, we sizzled.

He told me about his divorce. At the time, he was a stay-at-home dad. "She called me from New York the night before my fiftieth birthday to say she was leaving me for another guy. I had to fight to get the kids back to Maryland." They battled out custody of their children, ages two and four, and Arthur lost. The pain in his voice is still evident.

I wasn't there, I only know Arthur's side of that relationship, yet my instincts are on high alert. Arthur reminds me this relationship is in the past and I don't have to defend him. Still, still. His ex is a strong woman. I am a strong woman. Arthur marries strong women. I feel my defenses go up.

******

Arthur has a messy diaper; I leave while he gets changed. A nicely dressed woman comes down the hall, sees me and says, "Mrs. Morton? I'm Kim, the social worker." After my divorce, I went back to my maiden name, DiCicco, but Mrs. Morton serves me fine in this situation.

I expel a breath, relieved to see her. Finally, I can get answers!

She begins, "Mr. Morton is supposed to be released tomorrow. I'll get all the paperwork together; make sure the doctor signs off on the release order. Do you know where he's being released yet?"

"No, I wanted to ask you what spinal rehabs you recommend."

"We send many of our patients to Kernan," Kim says.

"Are they good? What do you hear from people?" I want her to make this decision easy. Tell me it's the best place for him. Convince me this is THE place for Arthur's rehab, without any doubt.

"We don't often get feedback but I've been there and I know the staff there."

"What about NRH?"

"I'm not as familiar with NRH so I can't say."

"How does transportation to the rehab work?" I am clueless about all of this.

"We use medical transport companies. When I know what time he'll be released, I'll set up an appointment with them."

"How does this all get paid for? Is transportation covered?"

"I believe Mr. Morton has Medicare and they cover transportation to the rehab. I don't know how long they will cover his stay at the rehab. That's a question for Kernan."

Kim meets with Arthur for a few minutes, then Arthur and I are left to discuss his options for rehab, a decision we need to make by TOMORROW!

"What about NRH?" I ask him.

He echoes my concerns, "It's farther than Kernan and difficult to get to. You'll get caught in work traffic trying to visit me in D.C. It will be hard for people to visit."

"Any thoughts about Craig?"

"I won't have my support network out there. How would I get there? What if I get out there and they evaluate me and don't accept me? I'll have to be flown back here."

I wish we had more time to make these decisions. I wish Debbie had visited Craig. I wish I had a magic wand and could make the situation go away.

It's a Waiting Game

9

This world of sickness isn't mine. Not once did I take my children to the hospital. Not when my three-year-old son needed stitches. Not when my seven-year-old daughter broke her arm. Not when Kevin's fingers were slammed shut in a steel door. That was their dad's job. He could remain calm where I couldn't. Blood and guts and bones popping out are not my forte. Once, while my 14-year-old daughter held our Pomeranian dog so I could trim his fur, I accidentally snipped his tail. Blood spurted out in what appeared to be great quantities. I took one look at my daughter's face and said, "Only one of us can panic and I'm already there!"

I know nothing of the medical community, nothing about wheelchairs and paraplegics and next steps after an injury. Nothing to base a decision about rehab on except... except... except what others tell me. My intuition fails me. I'm too exhausted. I walk in semi-sleep, my body moving slowly, my mind thick and foggy, my feelings numb. Physically and emotionally shut-down. Decisions rest heavily on my shoulders, weighing me down.

Arthur will be released tomorrow and transferred to a rehab. I want him to have the best spinal cord injury facility in the world. But will he? Did I do my job well enough?

A decision has been made. Kernan is the path of least resistance. It comes recommended by this hospital. I call the social worker, "Arthur wants to go to Kernan."

"I'll put in for the transfer and see if they have a bed," she says.

I didn't consider a bed might not be available. What then? Another thing to worry about. Another opportunity to pray. *Dear God, please let a bed be open.*

Earlier in the week I received information about a trauma support group that meets downstairs twice a month. A staff member I met with encouraged me to go. She said, "We're trying to build up a support group. It'll be good. You should come."

Why not? I need as much support and information as I can get and it happens to be this evening. I take the elevator to the first floor and find the room. I'm early and sit near the door (an escape route, an easy exit no one will notice.)

The gentleman next to me introduces himself, "Hi. I'm Tom." I have little energy for human interaction. I'm not in the mood for small talk, though I rarely am. Where is the line between being "nice" and taking care of myself?

"Hi. I'm Angela. I'm here for my husband who was in a motorcycle accident."

"So was I! It's only recently I've been able to walk with my cane," Tom replies.

Is it prophetic that we meet here? This gives me hope that maybe Arthur will one day walk with a cane.

"Would you mind talking to my husband after the meeting? He needs encouragement and support from someone who's been there."

During the forty-five-minute meeting, the facilitator talks about the support we will need and what is available. "You've all been through a trauma and we want to help with the transition."

When they ask if we have any questions, I start, "Tell me about the spinal rehab program."

The rep for Kernan tells us, "They have the ReWalk™ Exoskeleton Walking System."

"What is that?"

"It's a Robotic exoskeleton system that provides motorized assistance to help patients stand up and move their legs."

This is exciting! Wouldn't it be amazing if Arthur could walk again with the help of ReWalk? It might give him hope and keep his limbs from atrophying. They are dangling a carrot in front of us. After six months of therapy: REWALK!

The rep explains how rehab works, "Each patient is evaluated and an individual plan is set up for them. Six days a week, the patient receives both Occupational Therapy (OT) and Physical Therapy (PT) from our trained staff."

I am full of questions, "What kind of exercises will Arthur do there? Will he be able to use the ReWalk?"

"It depends on his evaluation and progress. They work on balance and building upper body strength."

"How long do you think he will be there?"

"It depends on insurance. Was this from an accident?"

"Yes, a motorcycle accident. He's on Medicare. Does that cover this facility?"

"It does, but I'm not the person to talk to. His social worker at the University of Maryland could answer."

I'm learning that no one person has all the answers. The salesperson promoting the rehab will not know about therapy or finances. That's someone else's job. It is a theme throughout this experience—ask a myriad of questions, gather information from multiple sources and try to piece together a cohesive medical plan for Arthur—all without a medical degree, prior experience or knowledge of the process. A roadmap to the process would be helpful here!

When the meeting is over, Tom and I return to Arthur's floor. As Tom waits outside, I tell Arthur about him, "Do you want to talk to him?"

Arthur says, "Sure, that would be good."

Tom walks into the room; they shake hands. It's time for me to go and leave the two men alone to get acquainted. I want to give Arthur a kiss goodbye but this isn't as easy as it sounds. I can't reach him over the railing. I drop the rail and lower the bed so we can connect.

Arthur has always been the cleanest person I know. He flosses daily and brushes with one of those electric spinning toothbrushes. He cleans the wax out of his ears and uses the electric razor on his face and bald head. He swipes deodorant eight times on each arm. I've never seen anything like it!

Since the accident last week, he hasn't brushed his teeth or shaved. Getting close to him now reminds me of visiting my grandmother in the nursing home. Or kissing my grandfather who always smelled like tobacco and dirty clothes, his stubble scratching my soft child's face.

When I walk into my home at 10:00 p.m. I'm exhausted. Our twenty-two-year-old cat Denim greets me at the door. He's a little fluffball that we've had since my youngest daughter was five years old. People who think only dogs are happy to see them when they come home haven't lived with our cats. Denim is an old man now, losing his teeth and slowing down, but he won over my mother who swore she didn't like cats. Denim refused to accept this and jumped on her chair by the window, squeezing in beside her. Eventually, mom would scooch over to make room for him. They became good buddies, the geriatric cat and my eighty-two-year-old mom.

I climb the stairs, walk into my bedroom, simultaneously kicking off my shoes and pulling my shirt over my head. With relief, I remove my bra, put on my soft cotton pajamas and climb into bed. The softness next to my skin nurtures me, wraps me in gentleness.

Nights are the hardest for me. I look at Arthur's side of the bed. Sad, so sad. I miss him. Simply. No matter what he's done or didn't do, no matter what arguments we've had or what lay unresolved, I miss him in my bed spooning as we fall asleep. I miss him in the morning when I'm having coffee.

Friday morning, the day he is to be released, I call Arthur. We've replaced our morning coffee together with a phone call.

"Hi honey," Arthur answers. Does he sound despondent? Distressed? Discouraged?

"What's new?" I ask. What I really want to know is, *Did I miss anything?* "Has the doctor been in to see you?"

Arthur's head is foggy from the heavy drugs he is on for pain. He doesn't always remember who visited or called. Doesn't remember what conversations he's had. He might not remember the doctor visits or what the doctor said. This is problematic. I can't help him, advocate for him, or ask the doctors the right questions if I don't know what's going on.

He tells me about his conversation with Tom after I left last evening. "Tom says I have to advocate for myself. I need to be proactive in my own care." Mmmm. This could be good or it could get dicey. I've seen Arthur when he fixes his mind on an idea and seen him on his relentless quests. When he was released from rehab after his knee surgery in 2014, he was determined to sign up for computer classes at a local community college – that day! I tried to deter him - it wasn't the right time, he needed to heal, he could register another day. I refused to drive him. He went knocking on several of our neighbors' doors until one of them agreed to drive him. Did they wonder why his wife wouldn't drive him?

My next call is to the social worker. She tells me, "Kernan has a bed available. We can get him there this afternoon. I've put in a request for medical transport. I'm waiting to get the release papers signed now by the doctors." *Thank you, God!* Momentary relief.

Because of my phone calls, I get into work a half hour late. It will be a short day. As I leave at 2:00 p.m. to meet Arthur, I call him, "Are you still at the hospital? Do you know when the medical transport will come?"

"No. I've been waiting a few hours."

When I arrive an hour later, Arthur is still waiting. No one knows exactly when the transport vehicle will arrive. I ask the social worker who says, "The order is in. They should be here soon."

I am anxious about getting Arthur moved before the weekend when things slow down or come to a halt. I send a quick email to my mom's prayer group, "Please pray that Arthur gets released to his rehab today, before the weekend."

I sit in a stiff chair in Arthur's room, waiting, a book on my lap, our topics of conversation depleted. "Has anyone called?"

This time he remembers. "Debbie called. She wants to fly out to see me." My stomach clenches. "She wants to know if there is a good time." My stomach flips.

When I spoke to Debbie right after the accident, she asked, "Should I come out now or wait?"

I told her, "It's better if you come later when he's in rehab. He'll be able to spend more time with you. There's not much you can do right now."

I have mixed feelings about Debbie coming out. I like Debbie. She's earthy in a good way, eating healthy and hiking, climbing, activities people in Colorado are into. She's naturally beautiful, her face similar to Arthur's, wide with blue eyes. Her skin is flawless, her shoulder length hair soft and blonde.

Where will Debbie stay? She's always been welcomed in our home when she visits, yet she stays usually with either Melanie or Cheryl, both mothers of her siblings. I don't know the family history or dynamic and have not understood why she wouldn't want to stay with her father and me. Is it because Melanie and Debbie have a history together? Or is there another reason I am unaware of? Melanie and two of Arthur's children live in Baltimore, closer to Arthur's rehab. It would make sense for Debbie to stay there. However, this opens the door for Arthur's ex-wife to be more involved in his care and recovery than I am comfortable with.

A troubling episode comes to mind. Debbie was in town for her maternal grandmother's funeral. While here, Arthur planned a lunch with Debbie and his two youngest children. I opted to stay behind, "Go spend the day with your kids," I told him, "You rarely get three of your children together. Enjoy!" Later, I discovered Debbie invited Arthur's ex-wife along, without asking him. Why would she do that? Inviting his ex-wife crossed boundaries, showed a lack of respect for me, his wife, and a lack of respect for Arthur's wishes.

But Arthur didn't speak up.

He avoided telling me because he knew I'd be upset that Debbie invited her without asking him. He has precious little time with his kids, which is why I declined to go. I was upset FOR him and upset WITH him for not telling me. The next day, Arthur shared with Debbie that I was upset, and added, "Angela is jealous of my exes."

"She'll have to get over it," she responded.

He's wrong. I'm not jealous of his exes, but the sheer number can be off-putting. He has two ex-wives and a third relationship whom he had a daughter with. Sometimes it's too much to handle. That doesn't include the ex-girlfriend before me that he wanted to stay friends with! I joke that Arthur likes to collect exes like charms on a charm bracelet. I knew about Arthur's past, yet chose to continue this ride with him. I also know he is faithful to me. I don't doubt this for a moment.

Arthur recently shared with me that Debbie didn't like the way I treated him. She said, "She disrespects you, Daddy." I what? Could that be why she didn't want to stay with us? Did he try to defend me?

I'm confused. Wasn't it disrespectful of her to invite Arthur's ex-wife along? Or to say, "I need to get over it?"

On occasion, I've been called out for my sharp tone, my delivery, although I'm not always aware of it. Sometimes Arthur thinks I'm yelling at him. The saying, "I'm not yelling! I'm Italian!" could apply here. I am a bottom-line person and don't always communicate as gently or tactfully as Arthur does or as he would like me to.

My best friend Connie, says, "Angela, you say what everyone else is thinking."

Recently a friend told me, "I admire your strength. To be able to tell someone how you feel and set a boundary takes a lot of courage."

Courage and an edge. Evidently my husband and his daughter don't agree.

He's from Colorado, where people seem to be more laid back. I'm from the East Coast, where communication can be more intense. I've said to him, "I'm not asking you to be less

Colorado. Please don't ask me to be less Philadelphia." I'm emotional. I'm Italian. I emote and have an edge. *Why did he marry me if he didn't like the way I communicated?* That's not to say there isn't room for improvement. But don't make me wrong for being who I am.

I am uneasy about seeing Debbie and having her too close to me.

While waiting for his ride to the next facility, the nurses help Arthur get dressed, examine him for bedsores and cover his wounds with bandages. Bedsores are the bane of paraplegics. Anyone spending an extended amount of time in bed must be closely monitored.

Finally, late Friday, the transport arrives at the hospital. Arthur is gingerly moved from his hospital bed to the rolling bed by the staff. I worried that I would have to carry all of his belongings - his water bottles, his clothes, his laptop - the many things he asked me to bring. Gratefully, everything is loaded underneath his transport bed and wheeled out to the van.

I leave the hospital to get my car and meet Arthur at University of Maryland Rehabilitation and Orthopaedic Institute, otherwise known as Kernan.

You're So Jealous!

10

Every day I work four hours at the insurance company, then drive to visit Arthur. During rush hour, it's almost an hour and a half. On the drive, I listen to uplifting CDs like Wayne Dyer, "Excuses be Gone!" or Byron Katie's "The Work." Occasionally I stumble upon a Christian station and listen to whatever is on—music praising God or a teaching on the Bible. It reminds me I am not alone. This is not a solo journey. God is with us and He is the God of miracles. It gives me hope.

After two or three days, I notice that Arthur is unsettled in Kernan. He is intense and erratic. He is scheduled for three hours of combined PT and OT a day. Physical Therapy helps build up his strength so he can lift his body from his wheelchair to the bed or transfer from his wheelchair to the toilet. His upper body needs to be able to support his weight, about 180 lbs.

Occupational therapy works on everyday activities – how to shower, how to get dressed. Rehabs usually have a kitchenette to teach paraplegics how to boil water for tea, wash dishes, and set up their cooking space to be accessible. Most rehabs also have a vehicle on sight to teach transferring from a wheelchair into the passenger seat of a car.

Arthur's schedule is intense and his pain excruciating. He complains to anyone who will listen, "MY SHOULDER HURTS! I CAN'T DO THIS EXERCISE!" When he left the hospital, we were not told that he had cracked ribs. That would account for the twelve-inch-wide black and blue mark on his right side. Nor did we know about the bone bruises in his left shoulder. When he rolls over on his right side, he suffers acute pain from his broken ribs and on his left side, pain in his shoulder from bone contusions.

During an evening visit the first week, we meet the head of the rehab department in the hall. The doctor stands at a rolling desk. Arthur tells him, "The pain in my shoulder feels like a knife going through it." A knife going through it. I can picture that and the pain it would cause.

"Arthur, I am aware," the doctor says, "We've talked about this. We can ice it and take pain medication before and after therapy. You have to ignore the pain and do the work."

"But I CAN'T!" Arthur responds, "It's too painful!" We find out later, much later – he also has a torn rotator cuff.

"We have to justify to Medicare your being here. If you're not doing the work, we can't keep you."

Oh! Harsh! Ignore burning, searing, pain? How can someone with broken bones have three hours of PT/OT a day? Shouldn't there be a sliding scale of PT based on the patient's condition? It's not the medical facilities or doctors making these decisions.

It's healthcare insurance companies. So, while the doctor's response is not warm and fuzzy, his hands are tied.

Arthur is not helping himself, either, by not following the advice of his doctor or his family. I tell Arthur, "You need to stay ahead of the pain. Take the pain meds BEFORE you have the pain, to stave it off. Take it BEFORE PT so you can DO PT." He is afraid of getting addicted to drugs and takes the least amount possible for his pain. It's only been a week and a half since the accident, too soon to be weaned off the medication.

I've noticed something else that concerns me. The pain meds are affecting his brain, his decisions. He's a different person and it's scary to watch. Arthur normally displays a calm demeanor. This Arthur is amped up, everything a crisis. His voice is loud, intensified, his body leans forward, tense as he tells me his concerns. I can't tell what to take seriously and what he imagines is serious. I mention his behavior to our friend Nancy.

"Everything has the same importance to him," she says, "He can't tell the difference in priority between his underwear and his stitches. Don't let it bother you." Good advice. I can't follow it.

In his intensity, Arthur is demanding. During his first few days in rehab, he calls me several times a day asking for bottled spring water. He refuses to drink water provided by the hospital. "I can't drink the water here! It's full of contaminants and it tastes terrible! I need spring water!"

I sigh inwardly, helpless, the weight of responsibility already heavy on my shoulders. I cannot reason with him. "OK, I'll bring water up after work." The extra stop increases an already long drive by putting me in the thick of rush hour heading up to Baltimore.

Daily, Arthur gives me a laundry list– protein drinks, water bottles, vitamins. His hat (where is he going?), his wallet (is he shopping?), a CD player (he rarely listens to music at home.) I bring what I can carry each day, aware that whatever goes into his room now will need to be moved out of his room later. And who will be doing that?

But I want him to be comfortable. He's lost so much already. I get it, he is trying to control what he can – water, protein shakes.

Today, I leave work at 4:00. Arthur calls me around 5:30, "Where are you?"

"I stopped for water. I'm on my way. I'll be there in twenty minutes."

If I'm not quick enough to answer, if I can't get to the hospital immediately, he reaches out to family members, my kids, his kids. When they don't respond quickly, he calls friends, neighbors and his ex -wife.

My daughter calls me one rainy morning, "Arthur wants me to bring him water bottles. He is trying to convince me to put my two babies in the car in the rain, and take them out of the car in the rain to bring him water!"

"He asked me to do it and I said I would!" I squeeze my eyes shut and shake my head, weary from the battle while my heart pumps faster and my stomach clenches, ready to defend my daughter from my husband's request.

When I arrive in his room, a case of water is already there. "Where did the water come from?" I ask him.

"Melanie," he says. His ex-wife. I heave a heavy sigh, my shoulders collapse, my head hangs on my chest. I rushed for nothing; my gift is redundant. My time was wasted.

Another day he asks me for sweatpants. Then he texts my son-in-law for sweat pants. My daughter Ashley calls and tells me she will buy sweatpants for Arthur.

When I get to the room, he has a pair of sweatpants and a blue zippered jacket. His ex-wife brought them.

He asks for blankets because he's cold. Don't they have blankets at rehab? I load a blanket into the car and bring it after work. When I walk in, a soft purple blanket is covering him on his bed. "Where did this come from?"

"Melanie stopped by and brought it." The ex-wife. Again.

"But you asked me to bring it."

"Well, I was freezing cold and you couldn't get here until late!" Of course not, because I was working and your ex-wife doesn't have a nine-to-five job.

"Arthur, please stop asking your ex-wife to bring you things."

"You're so jealous!" he yells at me. Jealous of his ex? No. She has nothing on me. I am upset that my husband feels the need to reach out to his ex. I am hurt that he is choosing to ignore my feelings and continues to ask her for things he wants.

One day he tells me, "I need a little pillow for my back. It hurts when I'm in the wheelchair. A little pillow would help."

"OK, I'll look around for one." We have plenty of pillows. Pillows are a cheap luxury. I search for one small enough to fit between him and the back of the wheelchair. Fluffy and firm bed pillows, square pillows the color of lemongrass, too big. If I can't find one, I'll stop at the store for one.

When I arrive at his room after work, a little pink heart pillow is on his bed. I sit quietly on the empty bed in his room until the nurse leaves. I give Arthur a hello kiss on the cheek. I can't wait any longer, "Where did you get this?" I point to the pillow.

"Melanie brought it."

"Your ex-wife brought you a pink heart pillow?"

"It doesn't mean anything."

"You asked me to bring it."

"I couldn't wait! She lives closer than you do!"

"And that's my fault, how?" Standing a few feet away from him, I take a deep breath and say, "I'm asking you to stop calling Melanie."

"I can't honor that."

"Arthur, if you're going to continue to ask your ex-wife to help with your care, I have to back out. It's too painful for me."

When I share my frustration with friends they say, "Let someone else bring him things! Give yourself a break!" I know how to ask for help. I'm not trying to be superwoman. I'm trying to be a wife. A good wife. A faithful wife. One who shows up for her husband. I feel displaced, disrespected and discouraged. Arthur asks the same things of both me and his ex-wife. She gets to be the hero because she gets to the hospital first. I get to be exhausted.

Where, oh where is the quiet life I dreamed of? A simple life with no drama at this stage. Arthur and I, enjoying this phase in our lives after our kids were grown. Was I really so naïve? At this age? Or was I just optimistically hopeful?

Is Arthur Moving Back?

11

After Arthur's accident, my son said he would build a ramp into the house. I could curtain off the dining room and turn it into a bedroom. He'd be mobile on the first level, able to move to the living room, kitchen, breakfast room, and onto the deck.

A bed on the main level is not unprecedented in my family. Both my grandmother and my grandfather had beds in the kitchens of their houses. Aunt Lucy turned her dining room into a bedroom for her mother-in-law, and my dad had a hospital bed in the dining room for the last few weeks of his life.

Mom would be with Arthur during the day while I work. My brother said, "This could be good for both of them. It would give mom a purpose and Arthur would have someone with him while he's recovering." This could work for a while until we figure out the future.

I can DO this. WE can do this.

I stare out my bedroom window, seeing nothing as I process what Arthur just told me on the phone. I have been researching how to make the house handicap accessible so he can be released to our home, but I don't get a chance to tell this to Arthur before his phone call.

"I'm getting an apartment when I leave here."

"You're what?"

"I'm getting an apartment when I leave rehab!"

"Arthur what are you talking about?"

"I'm getting an apartment in Baltimore!"

"Why??"

"The house is not set up for me!"

"But Arthur, Kevin said he'll build you a ramp into the house. I'll turn the dining room into a bedroom."

"No! That won't work!" he says forcefully, "The house needs to be ADA approved before I move in and it won't pass!"

"Is there a reason you want to be in Baltimore?"

"I want to be near my rehab! And my kids are out here!" He presumes once released from rehab hospital, he'll have out-patient rehab at the same facility.

"But your wife is in Rockville. There are rehabs in Rockville."

He is not budging.

A few days later, we have another conversation. The mortgage is due and my paycheck doesn't cover it. "Arthur, can you transfer money into my account to help pay the mortgage?"

"I am NOT contributing the household bills," he tells me, "I don't live there anymore."

"Arthur, this is your home! We'll make it handicap accessible!" I reiterate, "Kevin said he would build you a ramp!" I'm grasping, trying to find words that he will understand, words that will penetrate. Words that will remind him we are a couple.

My plans and my concerns are falling on deaf ears. He has made up his mind. He is NOT contributing to the household bills; he is NOT coming home.

"You're not making sense! What about me, your wife? I still live here."

"I have to save my money for my apartment!" he says.

"So, you're getting an apartment without me?"

"Yes, you have your job in Gaithersburg. I need to be here close to my physical therapy!"

He is firm, adamant, unyielding. Does he want to break up with me before I can leave him? Is that what's going on?

"Arthur, what about me?" I don't understand. *Is he leaving me? Are we breaking up?*

It's a question I will continue to ask myself in the coming months. *What about me? Where is Angela in all of this?*

I feel lost, adrift, desperate to save my marriage as my life is blowing up.

"You can visit me on weekends," he tells me.

Now I am a visitor? *Oh God, what's happening?* My life is spiraling out of control!

He informs me he is going to be making decisions about his care. After his visit with Tom at Shock Trauma, where he was encouraged to advocate for himself, Arthur has zealously guarded his right to decision-making, vehemently advocates for himself, without any help from me, thank you very much.

Arthur wants to take care of himself, be proactive in deciding how he is going to live as a paraplegic. It's admirable. Except taking care of himself excludes me, our marriage, our life. He's a separate entity. Totally separate. Oh, wait. This isn't new. He has made decisions like this before the accident, without me. The motorcycle he bought? I wanted a trike, a three-wheeler. I understood the risks at our age. A trike wouldn't eliminate risk but I reasoned it would minimize them. He didn't agree. He bought the bike he had the accident in, a powerful 1200cc bike. I will never know if having a trike would have changed the outcome.

The drugs are affecting his cognition. Ever since he came to rehab, he is distressed, agitated. His normal calm demeanor is absent. He barks orders at me; he raises a stink with the staff. He defends people who don't ask to be defended. When a wheelchair patient couldn't get through the dining room doors, Arthur yelled, "They're not ADA approved!"

As a result of his willful behavior, one evening, the head of rehab and his support staff show up in Arthur's room. They tell him, "You may not be right for our program. Here's why…" Later, my son-in-law, who is a nursing assistant, told me it's called a "Show of force." It's deliberately planned to strong-arm the patient into being compliant. Arthur later told me he was scared, blindsided. He advocated for himself to stay in the program. It bought him some time.

I'm not sure where this decision to move into an apartment alone is coming from. Does he really believe he can take care of himself? As a recent paraplegic, living alone?

He tells his daughter Debbie he's not moving back. He tells anyone who visits, who talks on the phone. When Debbie is in town, she says to me, "I think you should make other arrangements. He's saying he's not moving back to the house."

Friends are asking, "Are you together? Is he leaving you?"

I don't know. I have no idea.

The huge mortgage payment looms before me. The big house. Taking care of it myself. I don't want to support the house by myself. I've done that.

When my first marriage wasn't going well, I didn't think I could financially support me and my kids. I had given up my dream career as a cosmetologist when we moved to Maryland.

Child support? I couldn't count on that. If he couldn't hold down a job, how could I depend on him after the divorce?

The year before my divorce, I started working full-time as a Loan Processor in the mortgage industry. By the time my marriage split up I was more confident. There is nothing quite like making money to boost a person's self-esteem.

A year later, I was laid off. I interviewed for a receptionist position at an insurance agency, something low-key, not too stressful. At my second interview, they told me, "You're over-qualified for the receptionist position. We'd like to offer you a position as a Customer Service Rep."

"But I don't know anything about insurance."

"We'll train you and pay for you to get your license to be an agent."

They were offering more money than I was being paid as a loan processor and paying for me to become an agent. I accepted the position. A few years later, a headhunter found me and I moved to a larger insurance company, nearly doubling my salary. I kept my beautiful home, paid the mortgage and supported myself and my girls.

I didn't stop to realize what a huge deal it was that I kept my house and quickly increased my salary until my friend Shelley said, "You've accomplished a lot in five years!" Yes, yes, I had.

As I hang up the phone from another unsettling conversation with Arthur, I remember the weight of all of this, supporting the five-bedroom five-level split, keeping up with the lawn and the snow removal. All that must be done to keep the house fresh – paint, power wash the deck, clean the gutters. The hardwood floors need to be refinished.

This time I'm not up to supporting the big house. I'm twelve years older. I don't have kids who need a roof over their heads. The house needs work. A linoleum kitchen floor I've wanted replaced for years. Laminate countertops that beg for granite.

A hardwood floor to lay in the family room, bare from having torn up the original tiles. The house needs painting, yard work and updating. I don't have the strength.

And then there's Mom. If Arthur isn't coming back, I'll need to take care of Mom myself. And the house. And my job. It's too much. I reach out for prayers again to my Moms' Group, "Please pray for us. Arthur says he is moving into an apartment by himself."

I try to discuss the house with Arthur again. I beg him to talk to me. "NO," he says, "I've made up my mind."

I'm losing my husband, my marriage. *What the heck is going on?*

Where Do I Go From Here?

12

I walk downstairs to get a cup of tea. Breathe. I need to catch my breath.

Arthur isn't acting like a husband, nor is he treating me like a wife. He's making unilateral decisions - again. Decisions that affect me and change my life. This behavior is all too familiar, however, this time the stakes are much higher.

I hoped for an easy relationship. I'd already experienced difficult. I hoped for a marriage of open communication, shared responsibility. Decisions based on discussion and agreement. I imagined compromise, talking concerns through. Enjoying someone by my side while we travel across the country, stopping at little inns along the way. Someone to fly to Hawaii and

Paris with and hold my hand during a movie. I dreamed of someone to dance with, explore spirituality with. My children are grown, with their own lives. I needed mine. I yearned for a companion to share my twilight years.

My friends and my brothers are celebrating anniversaries in the thirty-five-year range. What is that like? I may never know. In my first marriage, twenty of the twenty-four years were challenging. I desperately wanted my second marriage to work.

I didn't expect to be free in my forties. Dating. Without the youthful looks and pert, svelte body. Men my age weren't looking at me, they were looking for younger women. I had a discussion about this with a beautiful blond-haired blue-eyed friend. She said, "After thirty, we become invisible to men." I used to turn heads when I walked into a room. At forty-six I had to tell myself to hold my head high; I am still beautiful.

After my divorce, I believed if it was God's Will for me to be in a relationship, He would find me the right person. At my cousin's suggestion, I prayed to my Angels, 'Please bring the right man to me.'

The year I turned fifty, I attended a dinner party to celebrate a friend's birthday. As I was collecting money for the check, a well-groomed man came up to me, "Do you have enough money for the check and the tip? Do you need anymore?"

Later, I would find out that his name was Arthur. He was coming out of a difficult five-year relationship. My friend gave him my number. He called me on Labor Day weekend, 2008. We liked each other immediately. Our chemistry was smoldering.

I told Arthur from the beginning I didn't need to get married again. I was fifty with three kids; he was sixty-one with five kids. We weren't having more children together. "Why do we need to get married? You've been married twice. Why would you want to do this again?" A part of me wanted to be a part of someone else. Sealed. A part of me didn't.

We took a trip to the West Coast in October 2009 for the eightieth birthday of Arthur's mother where I would meet most of his twelve living siblings and assorted nieces and nephews.

"Are you overwhelmed by all of us?" they asked.

"No, I came from a large Italian family. This is good, comfortable."

I saw the Pacific Ocean for the first time; we walked on the beach, collected shells. We visited Muir Woods and Sausalito. After meandering around Ghirardelli Square, we walked to Pier 39 where the sea lions gather on the docks, flopping on top of each other, pushing each other off, sun-bathing. We ate a late lunch at a restaurant on the pier. Our table had a view of the Bay Bridge. Outside the window we watched the sea lions frolicking.

Seated across from each other, Arthur looked up at me and said, "I want to ask you something."

I looked up from my food. "Okaaaay." *What is this about?*

"Will you marry me?"

I looked at his face, into his eyes. "Can you ask me that again?"

"Will you marry me?"

"Yes!" I didn't know until he asked that I would say yes.

After lunch, we walked back on the pier. I called my daughters. They were happy for me. I was happy for me, smiling like a young bride-to-be again. *Someone loves me! Arthur wants me!*

We were in no hurry to get married. It would come up organically; there was no rush. Over the next few months, we decided on a June wedding.

The bubble of my happy musings bursts and I crash back to reality, sitting here in my living room, surrounded by boxes. Arthur isn't moving back to this house. I'm not sure if I have a marriage. How can a marriage survive these crises? The accident. Arthur a paraplegic. Wanting his own apartment in Baltimore. My job—more necessary than ever—is more than an hour away.

I pray. I ask friends to pray. I need to know what to do! The answer I am hearing spiritually is if Arthur isn't going to move back to the house or help me with the mortgage, I should sell it. With five bedrooms, it's too much house to handle. When Arthur hears this, he says, "I'm getting a storage unit. I'm moving my stuff out of our house into a storage unit."

Before we were married in June of 2010, we needed to discuss money, bills, and living arrangements. He still had his apartment, although he stopped living there, slowly moving his clothes into my bedroom. *When will he give the apartment up? Why is he still keeping it? Is it a failsafe in case our relationship doesn't last?*

Arthur wouldn't let me see his apartment. He wouldn't invite me over. One day I asked him, "Are you hiding a wife?"

Arthur laughed, "No! There's a lot of stuff."

A month before our wedding, he finally agreed to let me in. There was, indeed, a lot of stuff. Nearly every surface was covered. I jumped in to help empty it by our June wedding. He donated heaps, moved a few pieces of furniture to my house and put the rest in storage. I thought he had stopped accumulating, yet as I begin to pack up the house, I find stuff hidden – in crawl spaces, in the basement.

I stare out the living room window with my tea, pondering Arthur's announcement that he is not moving back into our home; he is getting an apartment in Baltimore without me. *Where do I go from here?* I am stunned by his announcement. Stunned he would make this decision without talking to me.

But he's done this before – made financial decisions without me - like the second sailboat and trailer he bought last year. Who needs two sailboats? I can count on one hand the number of times we used the first one. Shocked when I found out I said, "You bought a boat?"

"It's my money," he replied, "I'll spend it how I want."

This is Arthur being Arthur, but intensified on drugs. If he was unreasonable before, he is absolutely out of reach now. He is not thinking clearly or looking at the ramifications of his actions.

Where is this relationship going? Are we married or on the way to divorce?

I'm grateful I never put the title of the house in Arthur's name, though it was a bone of contention between us. Before the accident, I suggested we sell the house and buy one together, both of our names on the title. He refused. It will be easier now to sell the house without Arthur's input.

What do I *need?* I need to think about myself. Do I want to be in a relationship with someone who makes decisions without me? Who plans to move into an apartment in Baltimore alone? *Where am* I *in all of this?* Exhausted. Alone. Scared. Confused.

Chaos Threatens

13

Arthur's daughter Debbie is due in town on July 2. Debbie is a light in Arthur's life. It will raise his spirits to have her here and bring him joy.

Debbie and I have butted heads in the past and, since tensions between Arthur and me are already heightened, I am anxious about the turmoil her visit might bring.

My experience with Debbie is that she can unknowingly and unintentionally (I'm giving her the benefit of the doubt) bring chaos into our lives.

Debbie does what she does with the confidence of someone who lives her life not to please others but owns her choices. It's an admirable quality. But what if the person on the other end is following a different set of rules? For example, if Debbie is running late, she may say, "Well, they'll just have to wait." If I'm running late, my anxiety increases because I understand I'm wasting someone's time.

When Debbie is around, I can be sure my boundaries are going to be tested, crossed and possibly obliterated! Maybe spending time together will benefit our relationship. When I'm with her, though, I'm watching every word I say.

Debbie can be sweet and kind and incredibly patient with her children. And she can pounce without notice. She told me she would argue with her grandmother, a staunch Catholic. Did she do it to get a rise out of her because she could? I have seen that side of her; the side that wants to argue, to puncture the conversation, poke a hole and wiggle it around, an open gaping unresolved hole.

A few years ago, Arthur and I were sitting at Debbie's kitchen table with one of his nieces, a PhD student. Her father was paying her way through school, making it possible. I've been paying my own way through college one semester at a time for many years. Arthur has been less than enthusiastic about me going, the time spent in my relentless pursuit for a college degree, the money he judged could be used elsewhere.

Arthur was effusing over how wonderful it was that his niece was going to grad school. Listening to Arthur's glowing comments, I quipped, "Why are you so supportive of your niece going to school, but not me?"

Debbie jumped in, "Maybe it's because he doesn't want to pay for you to go to college."

I was shocked, "Arthur doesn't pay for me to go to school." Arthur says nothing. Debbie says nothing. I am having a slow burn. Why would she think that? Did Arthur suggest that to her? Doesn't her husband support her? What would be wrong if Arthur DID help pay for my college? So much is wrong with that statement.

This and other conversations have led me to believe that Debbie doesn't respect me. Nor does she seem to have a high opinion of me. Arthur shared with me that Debbie didn't want her children in our car because I didn't respect him and she didn't want her kids around that.

Wow! Oh Wow!

There have been other verbal thrusts, and I have no desire to get into a sparring match with her. She is Arthur's daughter. His relationships with his kids being tenuous, I will not purposely fray it further.

Shaking off my musings, I say nothing to Arthur when he tells me Debbie is coming into town. Nor do I reach out to Debbie. I let it ride out, nervous, anxious, wary.

Chris and Cori Visit Arthur

14

Sunday, June 28, 2015

Shortly after Arthur arrives at Kernan rehab, Chris and Cori, our friends from the cabin in West Virginia, pay him a visit. When I picture Chris, it's always with a smile on her face. Beautiful, red-haired, vibrant Chris is known to grow her fabulous locks down past her knees, one sheet of gorgeous copper red hair. Then she slashes it off and donates it. Short hair or long, Chris is lovely inside and out.

Cori is razor sharp with a New York wit. She enjoys reminding me, "I didn't like you when I first met you!" She describes herself as a hedgehog, prickly on the outside, soft on the inside. I concur, but Cori has softened since I met her at the pre-Thanksgiving feast at the cabin in 2008.

I am looking forward to seeing both of them. We laugh a lot when we're together. It's a long drive from West Virginia to Baltimore and a testament to their friendship and love for Arthur that they are willing to make this drive. Maybe they need to touch him, confirm he is still here, still Arthur.

Arthur began going to the cabin during a tough time in 1997 when he was going through his divorce from his ex, losing custody of his kids and starting a new job. Friends Nancy and Quinn invited him to the cabin for some R&R and he's been going ever since with his two youngest kids, camping, canoeing and swimming.

Before Chris and Cori arrive, Arthur buzzes for a nurse to help him transfer into a wheelchair with the help of a clever invention called a "Hoyer," a hydraulic lift. He is still weak, in pain and has neither the skills nor the strength to lift himself out of bed into a wheelchair.

When Arthur is in the Hoyer, he looks like a baby bundle being delivered by the stork, swinging in the air. A large piece of cloth with six handles is slid under Arthur while he's in the bed. The Hoyer is wheeled next to the bed, the cradle hanging from the boom overhead. The handles attach to the hooks on the cradle and Arthur is lifted up, like one of those games at arcades where you try to catch a stuffed animal with the metal claws to win the prize. Arthur is good natured about it, smiling and waving to guests in his room.

As Arthur scoots his motorized wheelchair down the hall, he greets the patients, the staff, waving and announcing, "I'm running for Mayor of Kernan!" I roll my eyes, embarrassed. He enjoys this kind of attention. I want to shrink and hide. It's his way of being a positive example to others, but it's a little over-the-top for me. When Arthur arrives in the reception area, Chris, Cori and Cori's teenage son, are waiting for him.

Chris jumps up and gives him a big hug. "Hi Arthur! It's

good to see you!" She beams genuinely glad to see Arthur. "How're ya doing?"

"Oh, I'm doing OK." Arthur replies, "Glad to be alive. It's good to see you."

Cori quips, "Well I hope so; we drove a long way!" My heart is full.

Arthur is bubbly, grinning ear to ear, happy to see his friends. Arthur tells them the story of his accident. "I was coming off the ramp where 270 and 370 meet. I wasn't going fast. When I went to turn the wheel to the left, the handle bars disconnected from the front tire and I couldn't turn it. The next thing I knew I was down the embankment."

After chatting a while, Arthur goes back to his room where his lunch is delivered. He doesn't want to miss lunch or have the tray taken away before he can eat. Such is the rhythm of his life. Feeding schedules.

The sun is shining and I suggest we walk outside to the peaceful meditation garden behind the rehab. In the elevator, Chris says, "He looks exactly the same!" Yes, Arthur looks like Arthur, a comfort to those who visit him. If he looks ok, he's OK. If he's OK, we're OK. Everyone wants to be OK with this terrible accident. It unsettled all of us. If this can happen to HIM, it can happen to any of us. We reach for some comfort, some foothold to stabilize ourselves.

We stroll around the garden, enjoying the warmth of the sun. Chris, a gardener, pauses to appreciate the flowers and reads their Latin names. We cross a little wooden bridge over the small pond and spot a large rubber tree plant. Chris and Cori sit on the bench under the plant and pose using the huge leaves as hats while I snap photos and we erupt with laughter. We haven't had much to laugh about since the accident, seventeen days ago. Laughter lightens up the heaviness of this still fresh accident.

Back inside we meet up with Arthur. I say, "It's a beautiful day! Do you want to go outside?" He loves the outdoors and it's good for him to get sunshine and Vitamin D. He agrees and Chris pushes him through the front door, up the steep ramp to the front gardens.

This property used to be privately owned and a historic mansion sits on the top of the hill. We walk the perimeter, stop in front of the mansion and peek inside the windows, appreciating the beautiful architecture, acknowledging that builders don't make houses like this anymore. We imagine ourselves being the estate owner, having a croquet party on the front lawn. I describe the scene to them: women are wearing long flowing dresses with pastel-colored parasols and lace gloves. They sit at white tables drinking tea in large fancy hats. *What would it be like to have the means to own a place like this?*

Behind the mansion, Chris spots an abandoned greenhouse. We peer through the cloudy windows while Arthur wanders off farther down the path while Chris and I talk about the future, the next step.

"What are your plans for living with Arthur when he comes home?" Chris asks me. "Will the house work?" *Can our split-level home be refitted to accommodate Arthur?*

"I'm not sure yet. Arthur said he's not moving back. He told me he's getting an apartment in Baltimore. The house needs work if I sell it. Arthur started some jobs before the accident and didn't get to finish them." It's still early, but my sense is I need to prepare.

The future is unsteady; decisions are being made without my input. The ground is shaky and uncertain under my feet.

Walking with Chris, a thought occurred to me that I threw out, half-jokingly, "Hey! Wouldn't it be great if we could have a barn-raising? You know how when the Amish need a new barn, the neighbors all turn out and in one day, a new barn is built! Wouldn't that be great???"

Chris laughs and says, "Yeeaaah!" in that way she has of dragging out the vowels, stretching out the short word, emphasizing it. "That's a great idea!"

"Yeah," Cori says, "We could do that!"

"Seriously? You would? Come over and help paint and get the house ready?"

"Yeah. Let's think about it and see what we can work out," Chris replies.

We wheel Arthur down the ramp back to the rehab, sit on the benches in front, enjoying the moment, the sun, being together. Taking it all in.

I have to leave soon to babysit my grandkids. Like my mother,

I don't babysit often. When I was pregnant with my son, my mother said, "Don't ask me to babysit! I don't babysit!" Arthur was the babysitter for our grandkids.

Arthur tells his guests, "I want to spend a little time alone with my wife before she has to go." They decide to grab a bite to eat and wait. It's good Arthur wants to be with me. Still, I don't trust it, uncertain of where our relationship is going, especially if he stays in Baltimore.

A short while later, I find our friends. I hug everyone, give Arthur a kiss and bustle out to babysit my grandkids. I have a lot to mull over; much to pray about. Should I sell the house? Will the barn-raising happen? Is Arthur not moving back? *Oh God, what if he's really not moving back?*

Insanity

15

Thursday, July 2, 2015

Debbie is in town and she immediately takes over her father's care. Arthur relishes this attention, gobbles it up. There is no ROOM for me here. When I visit the hospital, she is in his room. She talks to the doctors and nurses and informs me about what is going on. She INFORMS me.

One evening while home in my bedroom, Debbie texts me, "What role do you want to play in this?" There is no response to this. She can't be serious.

What ROLE??? I'm his WIFE. Do I need a role other than that? Debbie has become the Director in the play and I have a role. Arthur is center stage and he chooses his ex-wife as his supporting partner. I am somewhere in the wings. Debbie is directing it…and she lives in Colorado!

This is insane. How do I stay sane in the midst of insanity? How do I keep showing up and be the supportive wife when Arthur doesn't give me respect? How do I advocate for him when he doesn't ask me, doesn't need me and doesn't see me as an equal partner?

I shouldn't be surprised. Arthur doesn't consider me an equal regarding our finances. Before the accident, he once told me, "You're not my equal! You don't make as much money as I do!"

I can't argue with that. It is his money. However, it's not the kind of marriage I want.

I want to love him and pamper him and rub lotion on his dry cracked feet. Money isn't the only measure of exchange in a relationship.

Arthur is wholly self-sufficient, forging a path through mental determination. Shortly after the accident happened, my daughter, Becca said, "Mom, if anyone can overcome this, it's Arthur." But Arthur isn't leaning *into* our relationship.

I look at the text again. What role do I want? I want to be the point person for my husband's care. Period. I shouldn't have to fight to be the go-to person. It's a given, isn't it? Yet between Arthur allowing his ex to be involved and him turning over control to his daughter, more and more people are lining up in between Arthur and me.

Don't get me wrong. Debbie is smart as a whip and asks intelligent questions that pinpoint specific areas. She is well-spoken and more available than I am since I'm working. Still, there's a respect factor missing here. It starts with Arthur's lack of respect for me. Arthur sends out the signals. Arthur is in charge of the hierarchy.

So many people are asking questions, involved, talking to the doctors. Too much input. This current situation is chaotic, a loss of control.

Friends tell me, "Let her help! Let his ex-wife bring water. Let Debbie help, it's less you have to do!" It would be less work except he continues to ask all of us for the same items. And I prefer that his ex-wife not be involved.

There is no order to this madness. Everyone is involved and everyone is equal. Arthur is not delineating his relationships. I am not at the top of the leader board. I am equal to his daughter, his ex and our neighbor Rita, who drops everything and brings him water and protein shakes when he asks.

When too many hands are involved, details fall through the cracks.

I am losing my grip on my husband. He is floating farther and farther away as more and more people line up between us. I can't reach him. I find myself superfluous, disrespected, and flailing. *Oh God, how to right this topsy-turvy world?*

Pulmonary Embolisms

16

Friday–Sunday,
July 3–5, 2015

It's the 4th of July weekend! I love getting dressed up for the 4th of July—all patriotic in my red, white and blue earrings and a navy top with red and white stars. The 4th of July brings to mind my childhood with family cookouts in our backyard, horseshoes being played with my uncles and cousins. In the evening, fireworks! I love fireworks! I missed the family BBQs when I moved to Maryland. This year, Becca has invited me to the parade in her neighborhood tomorrow. I can look forward to that. Lord knows I need something to look forward to!

After work on Friday, I drive to Baltimore to visit Arthur at rehab. When I arrive, he is at physical therapy. It's like a party here! Our good friends, Charlie and Carolyn are here as well as Debbie, and Arthur's brother Chuck. We are gathered around watching Arthur transfer out of his wheelchair onto the mat via the Hoyer, looking like a baby swinging in the air.

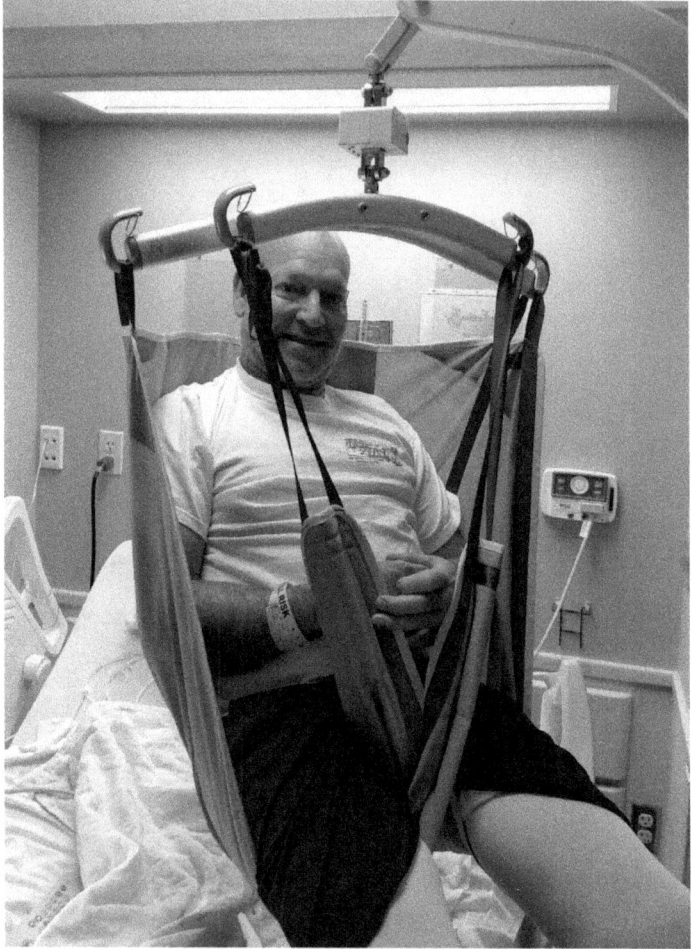

After PT, we all take a walk outside. Arthur is in the lead and excited to take us to the basketball court, although he's never played basketball that I know of. He says, "Earlier today a bunch of people in wheelchairs were shooting hoops!" Does this give him hope of normal? In his motorized wheelchair, he races ahead while we mosey along behind, unable to keep up with him. Arthur is on the move! He's intense. Intent on what, I'm not sure. He's not connecting with me or his friends. Charlie, Carolyn and I splinter off as we notice Arthur up ahead. Charlie knows the issues I've been dealing with since the accident. He says, "Arthur is the conductor! Everyone is following his lead!"

Charlie and Carolyn know both me and Arthur. I cherish their friendship and value their insights. With Charlie's comment, I feel validated. They see it too. I've been feeling like I'm living in an alternate reality. I don't know what is real and what isn't. I receive mixed signals from Arthur. He wants me here at the hospital yet he pushes me away emotionally. He puts me farther down on the list of people who have permission to discuss his injury with the hospital staff, behind his two daughters. He says he loves me but gives his ex-wife the benefit of the doubt.

I'm told by friends not to worry about the decisions Arthur is making. It will pass. Maybe it will. But maybe it won't. Maybe it's the new him, post-accident. Who knows? I've never been in this situation before. I've never seen Arthur on drugs, never had a life-altering accident to deal with. When I feel sad or horrible or painful, it feels as if it will always be this way. I can't see out of the fog to a future without this pain, this burden.

Arthur's doctors, the hospital social workers, his brother, believe he is capable of making decisions. Don't they realize how heavily drugged he is? He appears normal, speaking forcefully and definitively, answering questions and advocating for himself. He appears cognizant, but I know him. He is not capable of making healthy decisions for himself.

This high intensity person is not where Arthur lives. He can be intense, impulsive and not always reasonable, but he doesn't live there. He comes back to center. This is not my Arthur. I don't know WHO this is.

Charlie sees what I see. Arthur isn't Arthur. I'm not unreasonable asking him to not involve his ex-wife in his care. The validation changes nothing. Matters will continue to unfold; I will continue to be powerless, having little influence on Arthur, his decisions, his life, his relationships. It will get worse. But I am not alone.

Later, Chuck, Debbie and I go out to dinner at a nearby restaurant. In the car this thought flits through my mind: Be careful what you say. Approach with caution. What I say can be misconstrued, brought back to other family members. Choose my thoughts and words carefully. I am too vulnerable to spar. My place in Arthur's life does not feel secure.

Oh, how I want them to like me and for us to get along. Blending two families together is like waves crashing upon the shore, crescendos, twirling the sand in its salty midst, spitting out shells and jellyfish and seaweed. I feel like I am in the wave, being tossed about, relationships ebbing and flowing, sometimes high intensity, other times low tide. The earth is not steady under my feet. The undertow is pulling me. I am hanging on, the swirling eddy around my feet in the sinking sand.

Saturday, July 4, 2015

Derek and Becca pile the kids and me into their van and drive over to the parade route, parking a short distance away. It's hot, but not sweltering. Becca's one and a half-year-old daughter is dressed in an adorable red, white and blue ruffled dress with a matching bow she refuses to keep on. The parade begins, replete with firetrucks, girl scouts and clowns. This is a Mayberry RFD small town parade. I love it! The music, the festive mood of the crowd.

Becca has plans after the parade. I'm a little disappointed. I keep working on my kids to bring back family barbecues.

Becca has the perfect yard for it – a lovely shaded tree, plenty of room for the kids to play. Nope, she's not buying it. She says, "Mom! We didn't have big cookouts when we were growing up!" Ouch! Because I moved away, they didn't get those warm family memories I had and I still miss them. My kids realize I am trying to recreate my childhood memories. They want no part in it. They will not buy into my sadness and will not listen to me wallow.

With no cookout plans, I pay a visit to Arthur. Thankfully, it's a quiet day.

Monday, July 6

I'm off work today for the holiday. With Debbie in town, it's my day off from visiting Arthur. I decide to take care of myself today, rest, recharge. I begin with a session with a Core Energetics Practitioner. Following the accident, when emotions started stacking up faster than I could process them, I reached out to work through the myriad of emotions I've been having since the accident, zeroing in on what I need at the moment. It's part therapy, part physical movement. It's MOVING stuck energy. During a session, I may talk, cry or shake my body. When I'm finished with a session, I feel lighter. This is instrumental in keeping me sane!

After my session, I take a bike ride down the path Arthur and I used to walk. As I ride, I think, "This is for Arthur!" This bike ride represents Arthur walking and eventually riding again. I'm doing this for both of us.

Next, I go to a meeting in a fellowship I belong to. As I walk into the room, an old-timer in the group envelopes me in a BIG man-hug! Wow, did I need that! He steps back and says, "How're YOU doing?" He asks about me! What a gift! The focus has naturally been on Arthur. Tonight, I'm here for me, and my friends are happy to see me. This gives me a boost as I realize how much I need this time for me, this support system.

After the meeting, I check my phone and see that Debbie sent me several texts. In the car, I sit and read them. "Arthur has two blood clots behind his lungs." Ok. I process this. Arthur told me this morning he had asked his doctor to test for clots, explaining he has had DVTs (Deep Vein Thrombosis) in his legs before and wants to make sure he doesn't have them again. The doctor was dismissive and didn't order the test.

I badly want to advocate for Arthur. It's my strength - getting results. Give me a job to do and let me sink my teeth in, but he doesn't want my help—not for the important issues. He asks me for his electric toothbrush, his yearbook, and a particular dental floss.

At home, I head into my bedroom. It's almost 9:00 p.m. It's been a long day; I'm tired and I have to work in the morning. As I'm changing into my pajamas, I receive a call from Debbie.

"We're getting an ambulance; Daddy is going to the hospital." Oh! She briefs me - Arthur was taken to get an MRI. When they found blood clots, the staff immediately called 911 for an ambulance for Arthur. Why did he go down for an MRI?

"Do I need to come to the hospital?" I ask. My body is physically exhausted, my mind mush. I am emotionally drained from the upheaval of Debbie's visit, his ex-wife's involvement and Arthur's unwillingness to turn to ME during this crisis. I don't know how serious it is; the severity of the clots does not register with me. I don't remember that DVTs are blood clots often in the legs. I don't understand that if the blood clot breaks off, it can work its way to the lung, making breathing difficult and can even result in death.

I'm not sure if Debbie communicates it to me. In my exhausted state, I am not connecting the dots. Does she think it odd that I even ask the question? That maybe I should drop everything and rush up to Baltimore?

Debbie hesitates, then, "No, you don't need to come." I hear Debbie talking to Arthur, "It's OK, Daddy, we're getting an ambulance." I send up a quick prayer that he is okay.

There is nothing left for me to do. There isn't room for so many strong females. I have felt shut out these past few weeks. I no longer know what to do. I feel shut down and shut out.

Debbie speaks calmly, without urgency, to me. "They're having a hard time finding an ambulance in Baltimore on a holiday weekend."

I won't find out until later how serious the situation is: He was taken for an MRI because he's struggling to breathe. By the time Arthur was back in his room after his MRI, the hospital had called 911. The blood clots from his legs traveled up to his lungs forming pulmonary embolisms that could have killed him. The hospital was urgently trying to find him a transport and a hospital that was available. I didn't know any of this. None of it registered.

Later, much later, I find out Debbie called Arthur's ex-wife Melanie to join her at the hospital.

The Meltdown

17

Arthur is in intensive care at a hospital in Baltimore, wires attached to his skin, hooked up to monitors again. The doctors administered meds for the pulmonary embolisms; the staff monitors him constantly. He wears compression stockings on his legs for the DVTs. Because he is immobile, he has no circulation in his legs. Compression stockings help improve circulation and reduce swollen veins.

I send an email to our close friends and mom's group, my spiritual support, to tell them the latest and request prayers. We can never have enough prayers!

Tuesday, July 7, 2015

The day after Arthur is admitted, I work for two hours before visiting the hospital. When I arrive, he is surrounded by his kids. I'm feeling the cold shoulder. *Am I imagining it?* Are the kids upset I didn't show up sooner? Arthur's daughters have been given Arthur's permission to know what's going on with him. It's me having difficulty getting answers.

A nurse asks me, "Who are you?" I'm his wife.

It's been a rocky few days for us and I need time with Arthur. In intensive care, he's allowed only two visitors at a time so we rotate. The bed is high and it's difficult to reach him, the oxygen mask putting another barrier between us.

The next day I work until 5:00 p.m. to make up for lost hours. Throughout the day, I call Arthur - before work, at lunch, after work. Each time he is busy and can't talk, "The nurse is in the room." Or "I'm being changed." Or "They're bringing me my lunch tray." He has people visiting him, talking to him. Nurses and aides check on him, change him, bring him meds. There isn't ever a good time to talk.

10:00 p.m.

After putting on my pajamas, I sit on the side of the bed, shoulders slumped. Frustrated that we haven't bonded all day, I still want to connect with my husband before the day is over. I am trembling, my heart beats erratically, worry makes my breath shallow. Already uncertain of where our relationship is going, my insecurities are triggered by not having a few minutes of Arthur's time today. I am the one reaching out. He is making no effort to connect with me.

Debbie, who has been with her dad all day, is in the room with Arthur when I call. I am on speaker and Debbie can hear what I say. I ask Arthur, "Could you please ask Debbie to wait outside so we can talk?" I think it's a reasonable request, a few moments of privacy with my husband, a few moments to establish good feelings between us. We haven't spoken to each other all day. Debbie is always there.

"Debbie is tired and getting ready to go," Arthur says.

"Arthur, I need a minute with you. I have to go to bed, too. I have to work tomorrow."

Then I hear Debbie in the background, "Daddy! I don't think she wants what's best for you! I don't think she cares about you!" I imagine her throwing herself over her father's bedsheets.

Does she realize I can't rush to the hospital? I can't quit my job to be with Arthur every minute. I'm caring for my mom as well.

Debbie takes the phone, "Are you going to come and change his water for his Bipap machine? Are you going to make sure he has his Bipap?" The nurses aren't allowed to help with setting up Arthur's Bipap for his sleep apnea.

"I'm here all day," she continues, "I'm exhausted. And I don't like the way you treat my father."

"What do you mean the way I treat your father? I adore your father!"

"I should have told you how I felt before, but I thought things would change."

"What are you talking about?"

"You are disrespectful to my father. And I don't want to hear about this Philly girl stuff. My Mother is from Jersey. I grew up in an Italian family!"

I am stunned. Slapped. Arthur has shared one of our personal conversations with his daughter.

Arthur and I come from different cultures. I am an Italian from Philly. I emote. I have an edge. My style is direct, my responses can be sharp. I have tried to soften through my years of living in Maryland. If I still lived in Philly, I'd fit right in. But

I don't. When pressed against the wall, my Philly girl comes out.

Arthur is from Colorado, a whole different way of communicating. He speaks softly. Communicates in a round-a-bout way. I suspected he was trying to change me, that his way was better than my way. This strikes at my self-esteem, undermines my confidence. "I will NEVER be from Colorado!" I've cried to Arthur in frustration. "I can't be vanilla!" I love passionately, I create passionately. Being a Philly girl is a thing!

I am shaken by what Debbie is saying, "You don't appreciate everything I'm doing!" She is spiraling, crying. She is keeping me from talking to my husband.

"Debbie, I am sorry if you don't think I appreciate your help."

"Don't patronize me! I'm here all day and I'm tired and I want to finish up and go home."

My head is spinning. I never asked her to stay at the hospital all day, to stay until she is beyond exhausted. I don't believe Arthur would either. She is part of the reason I am not showing up more.

"Maybe I should have said something sooner," Debbie says. No, maybe you shouldn't say anything at all. My relationship with her father is none of her business.

My frustration grows as she continues to berate me. I tell her, "I don't get involved in your marriage. Stay out of mine!"

I try to get Arthur back on the phone. "Arthur. I love you. Can we talk?"

He says he needs to go. He'll call me back.

I get ready for bed, waiting for his call, shaking from my conversation with Debbie. Angry at her, at the situation, at being kept from talking to my husband.

Arthur calls back. "I don't like the way you talked to Debbie."

The way I talked to Debbie???

"I think we need a separation. A few weeks."

I am blind-sided, feeling panicked. "Arthur, don't do this.

Don't let your daughter come between us."

"I think we need some time apart."

"Well, your daughter got what she wanted."

"This isn't what she wanted."

"Then why are you letting her influence you?"

He is adamant. "I have to go." He hangs up.

Dumbfounded, I sit on the edge of the bed. His daughter prevented me from talking to my husband. He asked me for a temporary separation. *Did this really happen? What am I going to do? Is there anything to do?*

I fall onto the bed and curl up on my side, sinking my head into the pillow, feeling wretched, powerless. *God, what's going on? What do I do?*

I toss and turn in my bed. Although I am exhausted, my mind races. I am restless and soon, I get up.

I decide to check my emails. Debbie sent me a letter, not an apology. A lovely letter. I begin to respond, then stop, unsure of how I feel.

The next morning, Arthur calls me. "I said some things last night I didn't mean. I don't want a separation."

"Well, what you said was very hurtful. You let your daughter come between us. I have to think about this."

A short while ago, I was telling our friend Nancy that Arthur wants to get a house in Baltimore without me. She asked, "Do you really think he's going to leave you? In his condition?"

Yes, I guess so. I stay away from the hospital for one week.

Invaded

18

Saturday, July 11, 2015

Chris and Gary invite a group of friends to share their cabin in West Virginia four times a year—Memorial Day weekend, the weekend AFTER the 4th of July, Labor Day weekend and the weekend before Thanksgiving. It's always festive and restorative. Chris and Gary are having their post 4th of July gathering this Saturday.

I debate going. *Should I leave Arthur? What if something happens to him while I'm gone?* The cell phone service at the cabin is sporadic at best. There's also Mom to consider. She doesn't like to be left alone, although she can take care of herself. I can ask our neighbor Barbara to check in on her. Or I can ask our family friend Charlie. He's known Mom for a long time and lived with us for a while.

I need rest and relaxation. I need to be surrounded by friends, nurtured by their love, hugs and kind words. It's restful at the cabin where I can sit by the water's edge, nothing expected of me, nothing to do.

First, I need to find a ride. I don't have the energy to drive several hours to and from in one day. Leaving the cabin to drive home at night scares me. The road is gravelly, dark and winding. I call our friend John, "Are you going to the cabin?"

"Yes, I plan on it," John says.

"Are you staying over or going for the day?" In the past, Arthur and I have stayed overnight from Saturday until Sunday. I don't want to be away overnight this year.

"I think I'm going to stay over."

"Ok, if I get a ride back, can you give me a ride to the cabin?"

"Sure! I'll pick you up at about 10:00 a.m. on Saturday morning."

OK! I'm going. John will drive. Now I need to find a ride home.

I phone Nancy. "Are you guys going to the cabin this weekend?"

"Yes, we're planning on it," Nancy says.

"If you're not staying over, could you give me a ride home? I don't want to stay overnight."

"Sure, we can do that!" she says. Nancy has been such an emotional support during this ordeal. I call her when I'm having a meltdown and she adds a badly needed dose of reality such as, "I'm sure he has no idea what he's saying. He probably won't remember it!"

Saturday morning after coffee and meditation, I pack my tote bag– water, phone charger, snacks. A change of clothes, just in case.

I fill the cats' water dish; put a bowl of dry food out. While dogs scarf down an entire bowl, cats are grazers. They eat when they are hungry; walk away when they are sated. I ask Mom, "Can you give canned food to the cats?

"Ok," she says, "Are you going to leave the cans on the counter?"

"Yes. I'll label them too." I ask for her help to give focus to her day. I want Mom engaged in life, to have a purpose, to get out of her chair by the window. I leave a can of cat food on the counter with written instructions: "Put half a can in each cat bowl." If she forgets, the cats have dry food.

Mom watches as I gather my handbag and keys. In a child-like voice she asks anxiously, "When will you be back?"

"I'm not sure what time but after you're in bed." She looks at me with sad eyes. "You'll be fine," I tell her. "You can walk over to the neighbors across the street. Or call Barbara next door."

She looks at me, shakes her head forlornly. Mom has never liked being alone or doing things alone. Because of this, I cultivated alone time when I was a teenager. I wasn't going to let unavailable friends deter me from going out. I learned to be comfortable with going out to eat or to the movies or dancing by myself. I saw how miserable my mom was sitting home. I decided I could stay home alone and be sad or I could go out and enjoy myself. I've chosen the latter throughout my life.

Now, I brace myself against the inevitable guilt at leaving her alone. I would love to take mom with me. She would enjoy the cabin, the lake. At least the mom of a few years ago would. Sadly, this mom would ask me to leave an hour after we arrived. Through the years I told my mom, "Move in with me now, while you still have your health and we can still enjoy activities together." It's too late now.

John's car is waiting in front of the house. I pick up my backpack; kiss mom's cheek, "I love you." For the little reassurance it offers, I tell her, "I'll be back tonight and I'll see you tomorrow."

As I open the car door, our neighbor Rita, runs up to me, "Angela!"

"Hi Rita."

"Arthur needs some things. His wallet, some credit cards, his keys. He wants me to get them."

"Not right now, Rita, I'm on my way out." I don't want credit cards in the hands of someone under the influence of drugs. His behavior has been erratic enough without giving him ammunition. And what does he need keys for? He can't drive!

"Can you get them so I can take them to him?"

"No, we're ready to leave."

"Well, can I go in and get them?"

"Absolutely NOT!" I tell her.

"Well, he wants them."

"I'll take care of it tomorrow. I have to go!" I shut the car door, my heart beating quickly.

In the back seat, I will myself to calm down, to give over to the peace of driving away from chaos and confusion.

The drive to West Virginia is eventless. My head rests against the back of the seat, my eyes close and I sigh. When I peer out the window, it's a beautiful sunny day.

Driving through Harpers Ferry, long lines wait for large inner tubes to float down the Potomac. I did that once. It was terrifying! Such a large river and me so small on this float!

We arrive at Chris and Gary's and park in front of the cabin. We enter the kitchen, careful to shut the door behind us, to keep the air conditioning in and avoid Gary yelling a reminder at us! The kitchen is functional, with one large and one small refrigerator where we store the food we've brought for dinner. We all pitch in for the feast later when Gary lights up the coals. This time, I bring only myself. "We brought enough food for all of us," Nancy assures me.

John lays his dessert on the kitchen table. Across from it,

the coffee pot sits on top of the washer. As soon as the last cup is poured, another pot is made. Mugs with rainbows and flowers, positive affirmations and cute puns hang from nails on the log wall next to the washer.

It's a small log cabin with an open living room/dining area. Two bedrooms and a bathroom on one side with only a curtain for privacy. I fear someone will tear open the curtain while I'm doing my business or worse, while I'm standing up, my pants around my ankles. I prefer the outside bathroom, on the porch—with a door and a lock!

I'm happy to be here, breathing in the space, the air. I give red-haired Chris a hug. "How's Arthur doing?" she asks. Arthur brought me to this cabin and introduced me to these friends. Now I am here alone, without him, and my heart is heavy.

I want to say, 'He's crazy!' I want to tell her he sent our neighbor to get his wallet and keys from our bedroom. I want to tell her how upset I am that he keeps including his ex-wife in his care. Instead, I say, "He's doing okay. He stays positive. Rehab is difficult with his broken ribs and painful shoulder."

"How are YOU doing?" I ask Chris. I'd rather focus on my friends and their lives than talk about mine. A day without my life. Breathe.

Throughout the day people lounge inside on the well-worn sofas, talking in clustered groups. I enjoy sitting on the swing hanging on the screened porch, inside but outside too where I can see and hear the river, the birds, the trees.

People come and sit in the folding chairs by the river or hop on a huge inflatable tire and float down the river. The kids enjoy splashing in the water. I do neither. The river bottom is rough with stones and sediment. Fish swim around your legs, frogs hop on the water's edge. It's a little too primitive for me.

One of the first times I came to the cabin, Arthur wanted to go canoeing with me. I haven't been canoeing since summer camp in second grade! Eventually, I agreed to go with Arthur.

Before getting into the canoe, I put on my wide-brimmed straw hat and sunglasses. We slathered ourselves with sunscreen. Wearing my old water shoes, I gingerly walked over the pebbles into the water. Sitting in the canoe with Arthur, I was Katherine Hepburn in African Queen - the Queen seated at the back of the canoe while Arthur rowed us in front. At the rapids our boat got stuck; Arthur climbed out and pulled the canoe over the rocks. It was lovely and cured my fear of canoeing.

After dark at the cabin, a group of us gather around a rousing bonfire. Chris and Gary have designated male fires and female fires which determines who gathers the wood and who builds and tends the fire during our fellowship circle. When the men are in charge, Gary pours kerosene over the pile of wood and sticks; flames leap seven feet into the air, singeing the trees overhead and causing us to move our chairs farther back, out of the heat. Female fires are smaller, more contained, lit with wrapped newspapers tucked into the A frame of firewood and twigs.

Dessert and games often follow the fire, but not tonight. Tonight Nancy, Quinn and I head home.

It's 1:00 a.m. when I get home. Exhausted, I climb the stairs ready to fall into bed and sleep. When I walk into my bedroom I stop, as if a physical barrier is in front of me. Something isn't right. I look around. *What am I looking for? What am I sensing?* I walk over to the bookcase on Arthur's side of the bed, where he keeps his keys, his watch, his wallet. It's missing. His wallet is missing.

Rita has been here! My heart is racing, my eyes large, my jaw tight. Fury whips its way through my body.

I call Arthur, shaking. When he answers, I ask if Rita was let into the house. He says, "I called your mother and asked her to let Rita in."

"You what!!???"

"Well, you wouldn't give her my wallet and you wouldn't let her in!"

The neighbor came in, took his stuff and drove it to Baltimore for Arthur – against my explicit wishes!

I feel assaulted. My privacy INVADED. This woman was in MY bedroom! The disrespect. The falling at his feet when Arthur asks for help. Of course, they want to help him! They feel SORRY for him. But THIS. THIS is beyond being helpful. It is an invasion into my life, upsetting my mother and ignoring my request that Rita not go into the house. Arthur's request obviously trumps mine.

Sunday, July 12, 2015

Sleep eludes me as I toss and turn, fuming, frustrated, powerless. Restless, I finally fall asleep only to wake up early on Sunday morning. I sit up, fling my feet over and sit on the edge of my bed. Then, heart pounding, I call Rita's number. Before I get a word out, Rita answers the phone and says, "I am so sorry. I crossed some boundaries that I shouldn't have crossed. Your mom asked me to leave. She said, "I want you to leave now."

Good for mom! But this doesn't make me feel any better. In fact, it upsets me more that mom was uncomfortable having her there and had to ask her to leave.

When I talked to other caregivers over the past few weeks, they told me they took credit cards away from their family members who were heavily drugged. When I tried to do the same thing, Arthur sent a neighbor into the house to get them and take them to him. People can't seem to say "no" to Arthur.

Credit cards in hand, he begins to order crazy gadgets – a fly zapper that looks like a racquetball net, a long-armed device to take selfies, several wallets and special envelopes for credit cards that protect them from being stolen.

I am still vibrating with anger at this blatant disregard for my mother and for me. Later today, Arthur's daughters are throwing him a picnic at his new facility. His daughters planned it and they invited me. Invited me. They invited Arthur's wife to a picnic for him. As if I am a guest. A guest at my husband's picnic. They invite Arthur's ex-wife and another of his exes. Our neighbor Rita is invited as well as a list of people that Arthur gave them.

They did this to cheer him up, to lift his spirits by surrounding him with friends, but with Rita entering my bedroom, Arthur asking me for a separation and Debbie melting down on me, I decline to show up. I don't want to see Rita. I am too angry with Arthur.

Throughout the afternoon, my imagination conjures up pictures of Arthur on a rolling lawn, the center of attention surrounded by all of these women, fawning all over him. I feel like this picnic is a farce. A scene in a bad play. Another event of which I am on the periphery. *Does he notice I am not there? Does he care?*

Hitting My Wall

19

Exactly one month and four days after the accident, I hit my wall. It wouldn't be the last wall I hit. While on the phone with Arthur I look at the wedding photos in our bedroom. My heart hurts. I love him so much. Or at least the person I think he is. The parts of him that spoiled me, made me coffee in the morning, brought me a glass of water before bed, fixed my computer.

Our wedding day was such a happy day, yet it followed a stressful week. I suppose most pre-wedding weeks are stressful. The wedding reception was at our home. The house needed to be cleaned and decorated. The yard needed to be landscaped and mowed. Flowers needed to be picked up for the bouquets I was making for my wedding party. The food tables needed to be set up. Oh my, the countless details to be finished by Saturday!

Arthur has several meetings he attends regularly in the evenings. I asked him to stay home and help prepare for our wedding reception. He refused to change his schedule, "I'll help out before Saturday," he said. *When?* He was working full time and out every night of the week getting home around 10:00 p.m.

By Wednesday, when his daughter Debbie and her family came into town, I was anxious about getting everything done. Arthur and I took our lunch hour with them at his favorite park, Mattie J.T. Stepanek, where we took many walks during our courtship. When I left, I said, "I'll see you at home for dinner." Arthur had ordered pizza and I was last to arrive home. I looked in the box and it was empty. Empty. No one had saved a piece of pizza for me. This was significant because on several occasions, I had told Arthur that when he was with his family, he forgot about me. He, of course, denied it. But here it was, in his face. There was no dinner for me. Were the situation reversed, I would have set aside some pizza for him.

That evening, Arthur refused to miss his meeting.

On Thursday, my dear friend Connie, whom I've known for thirty years, arrived with her granddaughter, Nikolah, who is my Godchild. Nikolah was a bridesmaid in my wedding party along with my two daughters. By then, I was so frustrated with Arthur that Connie suggested we go out to dinner. Without the men. We had a mini-bachelorette party at a local Mexican restaurant.

On Friday, Connie helped sprinkle tables and chairs in conversation circles in both the house and in the yard. With over one hundred people invited we needed many seats! Nikolah helped me with the bouquets. When he saw me stressing about the details left to be taken care of, my son Kevin, who was catering the wedding said, "Don't worry mom, I know what needs to be done."

And still, Arthur didn't help.

Looking back now, why did I take on the task of doing it all if he was unwilling to help prepare his own home for his own wedding? Was it a sign? Should I have called off the wedding?

How do we recognize the signs that are so egregious that we should stop and walk away? If we grow up in a household without good role models for a happy, respectful marriage, how do we recognize the signs? My parents loved each other, but they had problems compromising, respectfully disagreeing and teaching us how to resolve situations.

Still, on the day of our wedding we were both beaming. We have sweet photos of us slow dancing looking into each other's eyes.

Arthur and I have shared delightful times—honey-mooning in Sedona, Arizona, dancing at a Victorian Ball in Cape May, New Jersey, riding the motorcycle on sunny Sunday afternoons.

Looking at those happy wedding photos and remembering all of this, I cry. Mom is heading up to bed when she hears me. With a sad face, she stands at my bedroom door and asks, "What's the matter?" And I put my head on her shoulder and cry, sobbing while she holds me.

Why, oh why does life have to change so fast? My emotions can't keep up. I've been so angry with him for his hurtful actions and now I am miserable. Grief. I want the fairy tale.

God, I'm scared. And I feel alone. I don't know who to trust. I say a little prayer I learned a long time ago, "Oh Sacred Heart of Jesus, I place my trust in you." A moment of calm.

I Don't Trust You

20

New rehab facility, July 10–July 23, 2015

The pulmonary embolism health crisis is over. Arthur is stabilized. I begin to understand that health issues with a spinal cord injury like this don't stop after surgery and rehab. Health complications arise. Urinary tract infections from catheters, phantom stomach pains, the multiple times they end up back in the hospital from an infection because their immune system is weakened.

We are barely one month into this tragedy, and there is so much more to learn.

It's already exhausting. Add the skewed judgement of Arthur on drugs and the family issues and I am mixed-up, mentally and emotionally drained.

When the hospital is ready to release Arthur back to rehab, his former rehab declines to take him back. He cannot keep up the pace of three hours PT/OT, and Medicare won't pay if he doesn't meet the guidelines: the patient must show progress. He is weaker now than he was before the pulmonary embolisms. He needs a step-down rehab, more in line with his abilities. Instead of three hours a day PT/OT, he'll receive only one-and-a-half hours a day.

Arthur still wants to remain in Baltimore. Debbie is still in town. When it is time for Arthur to be released, Debbie asks me, "Do you want to go check out the new rehab with me?" Because of the recent incident at the hospital, Debbie's meltdown and Arthur asking for a separation, I have backed away.

I am not sure I am needed or wanted. I don't understand the dynamics that are going on. I don't know my place anymore. Isn't that ironic? I'm the wife and I don't know my place!

When the accident happened, we were married for five years. Not long enough to have developed rhythms and worked out the kinks. Not long enough to say, "He's taken care of me all these years; it's my turn to take care of him." We did not have the investment that comes from a thirty-year marriage. Not that I don't take our marriage vows seriously. I do. But this is a big ask in a fledgling marriage, especially one with the problems we are facing. We had been given a few challenges—losing my job a month before we were married; Mom moving in with us. Yet this challenge, Arthur's accident and subsequent paraplegia, surpasses those in scope. It's life-changing.

I'm not sure we have a marriage any more. I am not inclined to invest any more time or energy into Arthur's recovery, especially when I am being met with resistance. I tell Debbie, "No, I'm not going." Debbie goes to look at the rehab without me and, I find out later, she invites Arthur's ex-wife along to choose the next facility Arthur is released to.

The new rehab is an hour away—without traffic—from my home, easily one-and-a-half hours from work. Not that Arthur cares or has a thought about it. He is near his kids, his ex-wife, the not-yet-existent apartment he thinks he is moving into. This rehab has a cozy feel to it, less hospital and more inviting. Homey, with intimate rooms decorated in plaid sofas, coffee tables and magazines.

The first time I visit Arthur in this new place is also the first time I see Debbie since "the incident." The night she had her meltdown. The night Arthur asked me for a separation. She would have left town already, but Arthur wanted to see his grandkids so the family was flown in. In a phone conversation, Arthur gave me the date and time Debbie's family is scheduled to leave for their return home to Colorado. I wait to visit Arthur. I plan to avoid her.

I drive to his new rehab, hoping for some time alone with Arthur. Hoping Debbie and her family are gone. Hoping I can avoid an uncomfortable scene. When I arrive, Arthur is not in his room. Searching, I find him in the dining room. I also find Debbie sitting at the table with her husband and children. My heart drops. Why haven't they left? I want to be somewhere else. I want to turn around and leave. I am still hurt and stung from our exchange and the aftermath with Arthur and I. Debbie comes over and gives me a big hug. That was unexpected.

I don't know how to act in these situations. I usually retreat if I sense someone's dislike of me. I have no need to be in the presence of people who judge me. Avoiding seems the safest bet.

But there is no avoiding this. The next best thing is to act as if nothing happened. I begin a conversation with Debbie's kids, carefully avoiding conversation with Debbie.

I don't want to be here.

****

A few days later, I visit Arthur. It's just the two of us. I spend a few minutes straightening up his personal things, tossing empty envelopes from his mail, throwing away used tissues and napkins. While clearing his tray, I notice official looking papers. I lift them up, curious, heart pounding. They are authorization papers for Arthur to list points of contact. Debbie is his first point of contact, Donna his second. I am nowhere on this sheet! Did he do this at the hospital too? Is that why they didn't know who I was when I showed up, the nurses surprised to see me? Do I need to be listed as his wife?

I notice other papers too. Beneficiary papers. Not yet completed.

Then an envelope addressed to Arthur Morton c/o Dorothy, at her address. I look inside. A bank statement. Then another piece of mail addressed to his friend Al's home address. Arthur has been busy cutting me out of his life, one bank statement, one piece of mail at a time.

Has everyone been colluding against me? Arthur, Debbie, Donna, Al, Dorothy?

"Arthur, what's going on? Are you changing your beneficiaries?" I ask.

"Yes," he says.

"Why?"

"I can't trust you."

"You can't trust me?"

"No."

"Arthur, have I ever given you reason not to trust me? "

"No."

"But you're changing your beneficiary and sending your bank statements to Dorothy and Al?"

Through talking to him and sifting through his papers, I glean that he took his money out of our joint account and opened another account, which was sent to Dorothy's address.

"Arthur, have I ever touched your money? Ever?" I ask. We had separate savings accounts and a joint account for paying bills. My name is on his bank account but I never thought to dip into it.

"Well, no, but I didn't know what you were going to do."

What was I was going to do? Empty his account and run away?

He is paranoid – yet the only person who seems to be affected is me.

Shaken, I leave the room. This situation is spiraling downward. *What do I do? God, do I leave him? What should I do?*

I walk back to my car, sure that I am leaving, going home. I'm done. Yet, like a magnet, I am pulled back. I cannot leave him in that bed alone like this, his eyes sad. "*Go back,*" I hear, that inner voice, that way God has of talking to me. I return to Arthur's room.

This wouldn't be the last time I leave, furious, sure that I won't be returning to visit him. Again and again, I will be pulled back to his side, unable to cut the ties. A power greater than myself propels me to return to his room over and over, even in my anger and confusion. God has a plan. I just don't know what it is yet.

It Takes a Community

21

A few days after her visit to Arthur at rehab, I email Chris to follow up on our conversation about a barn-raising. Since Arthur insists he's not moving back, I decide to get the house ready, just in case.

"I'd like to move forward with the barn-raising idea! Can you let everyone know? I'll provide pizza!"

Chris emails me back, "Do you have a list of what needs to be done?"

I love lists! They keep me on track and force me to focus. I reply to Chris, "Here's a quick and dirty list of what needs to be done."

Then I craft an email and send it off to my friends:

*Many have asked how they can help me during this time.
At some point in the future, we may need a one level home.
We're having a "Barn Raising" this Saturday. This will be a
tremendous help getting the place ready. There is much to do
and I can't do it alone. Many hands make quick work!*

I list a few items we'll be working on – painting, weeding,
cleaning the gutters. I provide my home address and end with
THANK YOU SO MUCH!!!!!!!

It's done, it's out there. Now we wait and see. I mention the
barn-raising to Arthur on one of our phone calls. "I hope you
get some people to show up," he says.

Arthur has a way of unintentionally tapping into my fears.
He unknowingly finds the soft, tender spot underneath my
bravado and wiggles it, jabs at it, until it grows larger and
erodes my self-confidence.

I turn philosophical, "People will show up or they won't."
Either way, I'm no worse off than I am now. I trust God and
if it's meant to be successful, it will be. I let it go.

Later in the day, I receive my first positive response to my
email! "I plan to come over for a couple of hours." Yes!!!

One by one, friends reply, "I can be there in the morning,"
or "I can come for a few hours."

It's a go! I turn my attention to my list for Saturday – paint
and paint brushes, tape, supplies like drop clothes, ladders, and
large trash bags.

I have been working four hours a day from 10:00 a.m. to
2:00 p.m. This week I return to my regular hours of 10:00 a.m.
to 4:00 p.m. With visits to Arthur, it doesn't leave me much
time to prepare for Saturday.

At the drugstore, I buy a large piece of poster board. This
will work brilliantly for Saturday. At home, I take a thick black
marker and list each job: weed and mulch the front and back
yard, paint the bathroom door, etc. Each person can choose

the job they want. I have a good, solid core group of volunteers.

On Saturday morning, they trickle in one by one. As more people come through the door, I have a moment of panic. *Are there enough jobs?* I needn't have worried. There is plenty to do.

My son-in-law picked up 10 bags of mulch for me ready to go after the weeding. The gardeners naturally gravitate towards yard work. They disperse, shovels and gloves in hand, some to the front of the house, others to the backyard.

I'm not a gardener. Unlike my mother, I don't have a green thumb. The former owner of my home planted perennials-daffodils, hostas, azaleas, that miraculously bloom annually without my aid.

Upstairs, in Arthur's office, I tell Cori, "Arthur said he's moving his stuff into a storage unit. He asked for help packing it up."

This bright sunny room was my daughter Becca's. When she got married, the room stayed as it was. Until Arthur came along. When we moved in together, I offered him the smallest bedroom for his office. It was unfurnished and available. Becca's room, though larger, needed work. I also had concerns about Arthur's undiagnosed hoarding tendencies. A bigger space means more room for more stuff.

I can't function in clutter. I need a neat, clean space. Arthur agreed to respect that. He wasn't proud of the disaster his apartment was and although he didn't have the skill set to keep his own place neat, he had a desire for order.

Over several months, Arthur began complaining that he had the smallest room in the house. The larger bedroom is "two feet larger than my room!" Yes, he measured it. Really? Two feet more? And we're having a discussion about this.

His small office was cluttered with boxes, papers, and computer paraphernalia that he didn't sort and organize after he moved in. He reasoned, "If I had more space, I would be more organized!" I wasn't buying it because of evidence to the contrary. His entire apartment had been filled; every surface covered with papers, books, pens. In time, he wore me down and took over the larger room, wallpaper half scraped off with neon lime green paint underneath.

As Cori and I stand now at the doorway to Arthur's office, there's barely room to walk in. His desk is piled high with papers; the floor is covered with boxes, computers and clothes. Wall art that never got hung leans stacked against a wall.

I give Cori boxes and tape; she finds a black marker in Arthur's desk to label the boxes. I leave her to it.

Painting is no one's favorite, but several agree to do it. Pat and John take on the kitchen and breakfast room. John is experienced at painting and immediately begins taping off the room.

Al takes the dining room. Arthur and I painted the walls pale green a few years ago, but we never did the ceiling. Al, a skilled handyman, spreads tarps over the table. I offer to tape off the walls before he paints. "Nah, I don't think I'll need it."

I give another friend a brush and a can of white paint for the bathroom and master bedroom doors.

Quinn brings his truck, ready to go to the dump. Nancy and I fill several trash bags with rusted paint cans from the basement. A basketball hoop with its cement block that Arthur removed and sat on the side of the house gets loaded into Quinn's truck with several pieces of old furniture. With so much activity in the house, my mind on overload begins to shut down. I can't think quickly enough. As I tick off a list for the dump, I realize the gas grill is still on the deck. Too late, Quinn has already left.

One by one, my friends ask whether I'm putting the house up for sale. I tell them, "I'm not sure yet, but Arthur told me he isn't coming back here."

"He's not? Where's he going?"

"He said he's getting an apartment in Baltimore."

"With you?"

"I don't know. He hasn't said."

"Well, are you two still together?"

"I'm not sure. I don't know what's going on with him."

I forge ahead getting the house ready. Ready for what, I'm not sure. If Arthur isn't coming back, I don't want to support the house by myself as I did following my divorce from my ex-husband. I'm incredibly proud that I was able to financially keep the house, yet I don't want to repeat it. The house is too big, there's too much to take care of. I don't have the money to fix it up, and keeping up with the mortgage would drain me. If Arthur's not coming back, I may sell the house.

It's lunch time, the house is buzzing with activity, and I realize I'm hungry. I have no idea how many pizzas to order for this crew! Five? Six? Ten? I ask Alan and he tells me, "At least six!" I order pizzas, chicken nuggets and several bottles of soda.

When the order is delivered, I look around for a place to put the boxes. The kitchen counter, dining room table and kitchen table are all covered with drop cloths. I open a folding chair and lay the boxes on top. "Food's here!" Several take a break and sit down to eat; others are on a roll and grab and go.

Looking around the living room, Nancy and Janet on the sofa, Alan on the steps, I feel amazingly blessed to have these friends show up. I'm humbled by these people taking time out of their busy, busy lives to lend a hand to me and Arthur.

As they finish their lunch, some return to their painting or gardening, others need to leave. I'm sitting on the stairs in the living room when my cell phone buzzes. It's a text from Arthur's ex-wife Melanie.

"I know I said I wouldn't post on CaringBridge again," she says, "but I did. Arthur has many needs and he keeps asking for a lot of things."

So, a) she is not a woman of her word. And b) why is she able to post anyway? I don't understand. Then I discover she was added as an admin on CaringBridge.

"I asked you not to do that," I text back, "I'll take care of Arthur. You don't have to do anything," reiterating what I told her before. "I'm his wife; I'll take care of him. You don't have to."

She replies, "Maybe if you spent more time at the hospital, I wouldn't have to!"

She did not just say that! I never asked for her help! It's Arthur who repeatedly reaches out to her, his kids and my kids. She lives the closest, and apparently can't say, "No." Now she feels burdened, blames me and decides to take matters into her own hands. I feel much judged, as if I'm not measuring up.

Doing for Arthur is a way of showing my love for him. If his ex-wife meets all of his needs before I can, what am I supposed to do? I feel displaced. Arthur and I have so little connection since this monstrosity of an accident. I wanted us to lean INTO each other for support, to be a team. Unfortunately, that's not happening.

In disbelief, I say aloud, "Listen to the text Melanie sent me!" Nancy immediately replies, "Delete it. Don't answer it."

I know Nancy is right, but I don't think I can ignore it. There is no right response here. I not only delete the text, I block her on my phone. *Who gave her my number anyway?*

In my bedroom, I call Arthur and say, "Do you know what your ex-wife said to me?" I repeat it, having committed it to memory. I expected him to be as appalled as I am. I hoped he would jump to my defense and call her out. He doesn't. He says little. I am hurt and angry. Baffled by his response. I don't know how to handle this situation.

Then Arthur sends me a text, "Can you please return the blanket and pink pillow Melanie lent to me? Please text me back when they are all out on the porch." A knife in my heart.

He cares more about returning the stupid purple blanket and pink pillow to his ex than he does about me.

I return to the living room to answer questions and check on work being done. I sorely want to lie down; so awfully tired.

By late afternoon, the front and back gardens are weeded and mulched. Bath and bedroom doors are painted; several boxes are packed in Arthur's office. The kitchen is almost finished; the breakfast room still needs to be painted. It has a high slanted ceiling with a fan and is not easily accessed. John and Pat agree to come back to finish it, though I know John is weary and is stretching his good will. One by one, jobs are crossed off on the poster board.

When everyone leaves, our friend Martha, a diminutive powerhouse, calls to check up on me, "How are you doing?"

I tell her how upset I am about what's going on with Melanie; the text, Arthur reaching out to her. She says, "That's Melanie. Melanie will be Melanie. You need to not let it bother you." *How do I do that?*

Martha is lovingly trying to support both Arthur and me, to be a friend to both of us as we experience the fallout of Arthur's accident, each of us experiencing it differently, with different challenges. We are not going through this together, as a unit. Today, I hang up frustrated. She wants me to…what? Be less reactive? Not take the situation personally when his ex-wife shows up on a regular basis? Not be upset that Arthur reaches out to her?

The next day, when I visit Arthur, I am still vibrating with anger from his ex-wife's text. When I walk into his room, he is lying in bed, phone to his ear, finishing up a call.

"Who was that?" I ask.

"Melanie," he replies.

"You called Melanie? Why?"

"I called to hear her side. "

"Her side?" Does she have a side? Isn't he MY husband? Shouldn't he have MY back?

"Well, I didn't see the text."

I reiterated her text from memory, "Maybe if you spent more time at the hospital, I wouldn't have to!"

He pauses a minute and says, "Well, she's right."

Oh my God! Are you KIDDING ME?? He wants me to spend more time at the hospital? I'm working, visiting him, preparing the house to sell because HE decided he isn't moving back. I bring him what he asks for, meet with his doctors. And he agrees with HER??? This cannot be happening.

Arthur supporting his ex-wife making a snarky comment to me is Just. Not. Acceptable. How do I handle this situation, when Arthur is siding with his ex-wife and I am out in the cold?

"Arthur, are you serious? You are seriously going to take her side?"

He refuses to retract or see how inappropriate calling his ex-wife is. He cannot see that I should be his first priority, not his ex-wife. Drugs or not, this is unacceptable.

After an hour, I leave. I am worn-out by him taking his ex-wife's side.

Bulges in His Back

22

When I visit Arthur, I regularly check his back to see if the spinal incision is healing. Is there an infection? Does he have bedsores? Today, he is rolled over on his side with pillows stuffed behind his back and legs to keep him from lying flat on his back. This helps relieve pressure and lessens the opportunity for bedsores. It gives his back air and helps with healing. I look under the nursing gown and I see a lump. No, there are two. I am instantly alarmed. I don't want to distress Arthur, but he does need to be aware.

"Arthur, do you know you have lumps on your back?" I take a cell phone photo and show it to him. One is about three inches long and two inches wide.

"Yes, the aide mentioned it," he says, "It's been hurting when I sit back in my wheelchair."

"Has the doctor seen these?" I ask Arthur. She visits Arthur twice a week.

"Yes, she told the staff to put patches over them." The nurse assistants covered them with a patch, center hole cut out. I'm not sure what the purpose of the patch is. Is it padding to make it hurt less when he leans against it?

"But what's it from?" No one knows. The areas under the patches are black and blue.

Then Arthur says, "The doctor doesn't have my records from Shock Trauma." Why doesn't she have records? Isn't this standard procedure? Was his current doctor supposed to request records from Shock Trauma? I'm confused. Did I think there was a magic medical bank in the sky that transmits this information? What is the procedure for this situation?

My eyebrows are knit together as I puzzle this out. These bulges are not supposed to be there.

I continue to monitor them and, over the next few days, the appearance of the lumps shifts, becoming a little more pronounced or a little wider and flatter. Arthur talks to the doctor about the bumps. She says, "I'm not a surgical doctor."

Monday, July 20, 2015

When I visit Arthur, he tells me the bulges are terribly uncomfortable both on his back and in his wheelchair. I ask the nurse-on-duty about them, expressing my concern that the doctor hasn't acted on them. She says, "If the doctor was concerned, she would say something." I'm not convinced. These lumps are a problem and, as little as I know about spinal injuries, I know these are not normal.

Arthur has been sweating profusely through his shirts and

gowns. When I'm here, I change his garments and buzz the aides to change his bed sheets. *What happens when I'm not here?*

Are the sweats from the bulges in his back? *Why isn't anyone taking me seriously?*

I call the doctor and leave several messages. She doesn't return my calls.

The bumps are hard to the touch. Arthur and I agree they should be looked at by the team who operated on him, but Arthur doesn't remember the doctor's name. I'm not sure I ever knew it. Arthur's daughter Donna volunteers to find out.

Later, she gives Arthur the doctor's phone number. The release papers from Shock Trauma show that Arthur should have made a follow-up appointment for his spine. He either didn't read what he signed or he didn't remember. I never saw them.

This is the problem when too many people are involved in Arthur's care. This important detail slipped through the cracks.

Arthur calls the surgeon's office and makes an appointment. How will he get there? It wasn't long ago that he could hop behind the wheel of the car and drive himself. Now it's an expensive, complicated issue. He schedules a private medical ambulance to transport him. It's a $600.00 expense and Medicare doesn't cover it. We are beginning to have a sense of the financial impact of this accident.

I have already taken too much time off of work so I cannot accompany him to the doctor's office. Arthur and I are still on shaky ground. I am still not sure where my place is.

Arthur calls me at work after he sees the surgeon and says, "The news is not good." Though this rarely happens, his x-rays show the screws came loose on the hardware in his back. From the doctor's office, Arthur is sent directly to Shock Trauma Hospital for another surgery. I'm glad I insisted he get checked out.

Prior to his surgery the next morning, the doctor explains that Arthur will need two surgeries to repair his hardware – one on his back and another from the front, putting in a "cage" to protect the part of his spinal cord that is protruding.

Arthur hasn't fully healed from his surgeries last month and now he has two more. Four surgeries in one month and a trip to the ER for pulmonary embolisms. With each surgery, he is back on pain medication. His progress is set back from his physical and occupational therapy. He loses more weight because he has no appetite. His face is gaunt; he can barely lift his arms.

Downsizing

23

Saturday, July 25, 2015

Since the barn-raising, and Arthur's determination not to come back to our house, I feel propelled to move forward preparing the house to sell. I begin collecting items around the house I am ready to let go of - a few quaint tables, several lamps.

Over the past sixteen years, many people, including renters, have moved in and out of my home and each has left something behind. Arthur and I combined households—two sets of everything. Then Mom moved in with her books and bed and chair by the window. My kids have married and moved out leaving some of their past behind – stuffed animals, mementos, baseball cards. Every room is full, including the attic and the teen room/basement!

"I heard you are emptying out the shed," Arthur texts. *Who told him? Does he have spies?* "Do not throw out things related to the boat, my car or camping. I'll have someone come by to pick them up." Right, because he'll need that camping stuff for the camping trips he never wanted to go on with me. Being an experienced camper since taking my kids each summer, I asked him several times to go camping with me and he steadfastly refused saying it was too much work. *What then, did he need camping equipment for?*

I shuffle through my closets, looking for excess. How many bedspreads does one person need? How many sets of sheets? Jackets? Table covers? I decide to have a yard sale. If Arthur isn't contributing to the mortgage, I need to raise money to help pay for it until I sell. If I am downsizing, I need to declutter. If I'm selling the house, I need to get it ready to show. That means removing excess and making it appear more spacious.

I reach out to my friends again, "If you can spare one hour to help with my yard sale, I would appreciate it."

It's an indoor sale because I have big pieces of furniture—the dining room table my mom's fiancée gave me, a green sofa I inherited from a neighbor. Smaller items are spread out in the living room, dining room and kitchen as well as the family room. On Saturday, doors open at 8:00 a.m. and, with the help of many friends, we are finished by noon. The sale nets $750.00. A good chunk towards my $1,800 mortgage.

Sunday, July 26, 2015

Sitting on my deck in my beautiful gazebo. An oasis in the middle of crisis. It's peaceful here listening to the birds tweeting, crickets chirping. Seeing the tree branches lazily waving. A black lab playfully chases a small brown terrier in the yard behind mine.

Yet my mind whirls and twirls and buzzes. The grass needs mowing. My neighbor's yard looks like a smooth green blanket compared to my overgrown shaggy lawn.

Can I take my gazebo with me? Will I have a place to put it? Will I EVER have one again?

I call my long-time friend Connie and I cry as we talk. "I'm so sad. I miss my life. I don't know what's going to happen." Connie and I have been through many crises together. Divorce, financial problems and death. And what is this if not a death? The death of life as I knew it. The death of dreams Arthur and I had.

When I go back inside the house, I notice the empty space in my dining room where the table that I sold today used to be. That table hosted many memories over the past fifteen years. The Feast of the Seven Fishes on Christmas Eve with my antique Lenox dishes and pink crystal goblets, the table extending well into the living room to accommodate all the extra guests invited each year. Easter and Christmas brunch, Thanksgiving dinners. And everyday living, too, as we often ate our daily meals here.

Yet in the empty space, I can begin to breathe again. Life is moving forward.

The Phone Call
24

It's around 10:00 a.m., Monday morning. I'm sitting at my desk at work when my cell phone buzzes. My brother Francis' name displays on the caller ID. I don't usually take personal calls, but since Arthur's accident, sometimes they are necessary.

At sixty years old, Francis is three years older than me. Until Mom moved in with me, he shouldered most of the responsibility of my mother's care since my dad died in 1997 because he lived closest to her. He would visit her weekly, take her food shopping and do small repairs in the row-home mom lived in in Philadelphia. He made sure her taxes were paid and balanced her checkbook, no easy feat since mom had no money sense.

"What's going on with the house?" he asks without much

preamble.

I'm running through my mind why he would be calling, where this is leading. "Arthur says he isn't moving back and he's not contributing to the household expenses anymore. I don't have the money to take care of this big house anymore. I'm thinking of selling it." Maybe I should have said, "Nothing much." Maybe it would have changed the outcome.

"That's what I heard. I wanted to confirm it with you." My brothers and I don't talk much. He must have heard this through our other brother Al, whom I spoke with recently.

"If you're selling the house, I need to get mom out of there. There's an assisted living place near me with a room available and I'm going to look at it this week."

Wait. *What?* Panic is rising from the roiling in my stomach to the pounding in my chest settling in my head as rockets explode. I don't, as a rule, think quickly on my feet. I am a processor. I am not at a place to discuss this and I cannot wrap my head around what he is saying. This is why I hold my cards close to my chest. One word, one action sets the dominoes tumbling down.

I figured I had time to sort my life out. Get the house on the market to sell, look for a two-bedroom place for mom and me. This is a huge curve ball.

It took YEARS for my mom to decide to move in with me. Years of listening to how lonely she was after my dad died in 1997. "Mom, you can always move in with me," I repeatedly told her.

Years of missing her on holidays because she refused to travel. "Mom, please move down while you have your health and we can still enjoy each other.

Years of lonely Saturdays when I wanted to go to the mall with my mom. "Mom, you won't be lonely here. There's always someone coming and going. Always places for you to go, things to do. Garden Club and Knitting Club and Seniors." It took one long, cold and snowy winter when she was cooped up in her home, alone and lonely for her to say, "I'll move in with Angela."

Albert called me and said, "Mom wants to move in with you." I didn't believe it. She'll change her mind. But she didn't. Not this time. *Was it just a little more than a year ago that she moved in with us? So much has happened.*

On the call, I ask Francis, "Why the hurry? It'll be another few months before the house is ready to sell."

"It's too stressful for her there with the packing and moving," he says.

"Francis, mom is fine. She enjoys the activity. I give her things to do." She sorts my buttons, models my bouquets. Occasionally she makes the one dish she remembers—peppers and eggs. Too salty as her taste buds have lost their sense.

"These rooms don't come available often. Sometimes there's a waiting list. This room is available and I'm going to look at it."

"But Frant (our family name for him), Arthur is pulling his money out. I'm counting on mom's income to help me with the house until I decide what to do." What I can't say, can't be honest about, is that I need my mom now for emotional support. I can't have one more loss.

"I understand, but this is what's best for mom."

I don't agree this is what's best for mom. "Frant, can you give me a few months?"

"I have an appointment with the social worker tomorrow." I have no say. I have no influence. My opinion does not matter.

My insides feel sticky and ugly. I feel threatened and powerless. It seems I'm always powerless with Francis. He's black and white, without wiggle room. He's not one to be open to options and possibilities. I have enough on my plate to deal with emotionally: Arthur, the exes, selling the house. I'm worried about money since Arthur proclaimed he wasn't contributing any more. I do not need this added worry. And he's my brother! *Doesn't he care about me?*

"Francis, I'm your sister. Do you not care what happens to me?" I feel small. *Why, when I am in so much pain, does he want to add to it?*

He says, "I do but Mom is my first priority." *Why can't he be concerned about both of us?*

And what about what Mom wants? Does that matter?

I feel desperate. Desperate to stop time, desperate to slow down this process, desperate to not add another crisis to my already overflowing life. I am coming across as though money is the only issue and it's not, though it's the most pressing one to me right now.

He is unwilling to compromise, to put off the meeting. I am angry, fierce, grasping. "Francis, I know we haven't always gotten along, but if you do this, we are done." As soon as I say it, I realize I know better. He's my brother and I won't be able to follow through. How could I? However, I'm not going to take it back. He needs to know how serious this is.

The truth is Francis and I were close at one time, when we were teenagers and for a while after he was married. I spent a lot of time with him and his friends, going to parties and dances. When I was old enough, we would double date. We went bowling together and to Beef and Beers. We danced, twisted and stomped. When my boyfriend broke up with me, Francis took me out with his girlfriend to Mayfair diner. On Valentine's Day, I found little gifts from him on the kitchen table– flowers or candy.

Naturally, it changed when he got married and had children. Of course, his family comes first, yet I still want my big brother looking out for me, like my dad did with his sisters.

Years of separation has left Francis and me unable to discuss anything rationally. I hang up the phone. I feel like a storm is blowing around me, buffeting me from every side and I am helpless in the center of it, unprepared for its staggering blows, raw, exposed and unprotected.

I drop my head into my hands, try to compose myself. I am at work. I need to set aside my personal life and concentrate on the computer in front of me, answer phones. I breathe, trying to calm myself.

First Arthur, now this.

I work through the morning, head spinning. *What can I do?* The only person who can get through to Francis is our brother Albert. At lunch I call him. "Al, Francis wants to take mom out of the house and put her in an assisted living."

"Yeah, he's anxious about mom. He wants her settled." Evidently, they've already discussed this. *What about me and my anxiety?*

This harkens back to my childhood when Mom would say, "Don't upset Albert, he has an ulcer. Don't upset Francis, he's sensitive." *What about me?* One time I asked my mother this and she said, "I knew you'd be fine."

I bring my attention back to the phone call and focus on the practical. "Al, I'm not going to have enough money to pay the mortgage if Francis takes mom out this quickly. Can you talk to him about giving me a few months?"

There are two issues here, equally distressing. First, Mom moving out, the rug being pulled out from under me. She is finally able to be an emotional support to me. And I need that now more than ever! And she is settled. She wants to be here.

The second worry, about my finances, is practical as two sources of income are suddenly stopped. I appeal to the financial decision because it's concrete and imminent. And because I haven't begun to process that my mom is going to be leaving.

I am powerless. In the pecking order of our family, I am at

the bottom, the youngest. It's taken me years to have a voice. Someone once referred to me as "a yappy little dog nipping at your feet." It's an apt description. I have a lot to say and no one's paying attention.

I walk in the door after work, tired. Mom is sitting in her chair. "Hi mom!"

"Hello, how are you?"

"I'm tired. Are you hungry?"

"A little."

"Let me get changed and I'll make dinner for us."

I swiftly drop my clothes and slip into my cotton nightshirt. I grab my robe and head downstairs. I pull shrimp out of the refrigerator for mom and leftovers for me. We sit at the marble table by the sliding glass doors, gazing out at the birds pecking seeds from the feeders. I cast my eyes down, dreading the moment that I have to broach the subject of Mom potentially leaving. And I'm not sure how. Instead, we exchange small talk, "How was your day?"

After dinner I sit in my home office to draft a letter to my St Jude's Mom's Group, sharing my distress and asking for prayers about this new development and its impact on my finances. I've been a part of this group since my youngest was a year and a half, making it twenty-five years. The love, friendship and prayer support this group has provided through the years has been solid and I can't imagine what I would have done for my sanity without them. Anxious inside, my shoulders tense, my stomach tied up in knots, I feel sad, afraid and abandoned.

My Mom's Group friend Shelley, comes over one evening to help me pack up boxes. She pulls me aside in the kitchen and says, "I don't want you to worry about money. If you need any, we can give it to you. You can pay us back when the house sells."

I don't know what to say. My eyes are large and seek Shelley's face. Is she serious? She is. I tuck this information away, holding it close to my heart, feeling wrapped in friendship and secure, knowing my bills will get paid, no matter what.

The issue of money is resolved when I receive a cryptic email message from Francis a few days later, "Check the balance on the card." He gave me a debit card that he loads with money each month to take care of Mom's expenses while living with us. I check the balance and am surprised to find enough money for one mortgage payment.

Meanwhile, the room at the assisted living passed my brother's approval. On Tuesday, I receive a call from Al, "We've set up a family meeting for Friday at Francis' house for 2:00 p.m." I quickly calculate this, accessing the long drive and whether or not I can get the day off.

"I'll see if I can get the day off and take mom up."

Then we discuss how to tell mom that we are having a meeting about her moving out. What's the best way to break it to her? I'm not worried that she may have a melt-down as in the past. Now I'm worried about her understanding of the situation because of her dementia. And will she remember it from today, Tuesday, until Friday?

"I'll tell her," I say resignedly. I don't want anyone to elevate the situation to crisis. I'll break it to her gently

Meet the Social Worker

25

On Friday morning, I am all business as I prepare to leave for the meeting in Lancaster with my brothers regarding mom's next step. In this state of mind, I can leave my emotions out. Eat, get dressed, gather water, snacks and my phone charger. Mom, who is already dressed, has always put her clothes on as soon as her feet hit the floor in the morning, unlike me, who enjoys lounging in my pj's as long as possible.

Mom sits in the living room in her chair by the window as it was in her home in Philadelphia. Mom didn't take to the transition to Maryland well, although it was her decision to move down here.

One of her laments was, "What am I going to do with my

dining room set?" Letting go of our life—our entire life—where we entertained, shared holiday dinners, dined with friends. Where we had engagements parties and rehearsal dinners and countless other celebrations. How do we let go? How do we finally arrive at a place where things no longer matter, though it's the things that hold the attachments—all the memories are etched in the dining room table and the chairs that my father reupholstered? How do we let go of a lifetime of love and memories? Let go of independence? Give up a home, a life. It is no easy task.

After mom agreed to move, Arthur and I rented a truck for a day and drove to Philadelphia to pick her up and move her to Maryland. We took what was essential. Mom's favorite wing chair and ottoman. A bunch of paperback novels from the piles of books overflowing from the coffee table to the floor. Books from mom's childhood: Nancy Drew Mysteries, Cherry Ames. Clothes for Maryland weather. It was a long, exhausting day and in the end, we had mom moved into our home in Maryland.

Who knew a short year and change later, we would be taking a trip to discuss moving her to a Senior Living facility?

It's time to get mom into the car. During the drive, mom asks me, "Where are we going?"

"We're going to Francis'."

"Why are we going to Francis'?" I anticipated this so I wrote down what we were doing and I give her the paper. "We're going to Francis and Judy's. We're going to have a talk with them. Albert and Ann Marie will be there too." I see her open the paper in her hand and read it.

I feel badly treating her like a child. Not being patient enough to respond to the same question over and over again. Maybe it's a kindness to her. She can read the paper as often as she needs to. I reach over and touch her hand. She looks at me with sad eyes.

After a couple of hours of driving and a bathroom stop, we arrive at Francis and Judy's house and pull in their long driveway. The living room is lit with sun as we walk in. Mom sits down in the chair by the window, the chair she gravitates to whatever house she's in. The front window overlooks their rolling lawn. I meander around looking at photos, noticing our grandfather's clock on the mantel, the ebony library table from mom's house fitting perfectly against the stair wall.

Al and his wife Ann Marie are already here. We sit together in the living room, uncomfortable, tension in the air. Mom is confused. Judy is in the kitchen doing last minute preparations for lunch.

When lunch is ready, we sit around the beautifully set table. Judy places meatballs, gluten-free pasta and a salad out. She is a good cook and an excellent baker. Dessert today is a delicious gluten free pie.

We have a 2:00 p.m. appointment with the social worker.

When the social worker arrives, we are still seated at the table. After being introduced to each of us, she pulls up a chair next to mom. A friendly woman neatly dressed; this is what she does and she does it well. Friendly business.

She tells us about the facility; she asks mom a few questions, "Do you know why you're here?"

"Not really," mom says.

It's surreal, this venture we are on. A jumbled roller coaster ride. It's not a ride I want to be on and I know my mom doesn't either. She is confused, like a scared little child trying to make sense of the world. I want to comfort her, even as I am filled with deep sadness about this turn of events.

Arthur's Birthday

26

August 2015

It's Saturday and I am having a craft sale to wean down my supplies. My button bouquet business came to an abrupt end after the accident. I have massive inventory left, thousands of buttons in every color, in teal blue, mint green, lemon yellow; and feathers, in peacock, pheasant, rooster schlappen; plus six drawers of ribbon, in satin, grosgrain, wide, thin.

As I decide what to keep and what to sell as I downsize, I use square footage as a measure. How much will it cost me per square foot to keep this in storage? The more I keep, the bigger the storage unit. Is it worth it to keep these supplies, this towel, four sets of dishes?

It's a slow day with a few crafters trickling in. I sell some vintage buttons, a few skeins of yarn. Make a little more money towards my living expenses, but the sales barely put a dent in my inventory.

Monday, August 3, 2015

Today is Arthur's sixty-eighth birthday. I sent him a happy birthday text this morning and haven't heard back. This worries me. We are playing by his rules and I am worn-out. After visiting him last night, I came home late, got in bed, then called him to say good night.

As we were saying our goodbyes on the phone, he said something that struck me as odd given the tension lately, "I want you to know I love you more than you know." Beautiful words. Musical words. Lovely words that one would die to hear. But why now? What's going on in his head? To assuage guilt about his ex? Because he thought I might be hurt? Because...

Our marriage vows said "I will love, honor and cherish you above all others." Since the accident, I don't feel honored or cherished. Loved? So much has happened. So many conflicts. His actions painful. My life is spiraling.

The injury alone would have been stressful on the relationship. But this emotional stuff depletes what little energy I have left, leaving me mentally and physically exhausted.

Under other circumstances, I would have surprised Arthur at the hospital today. Were it not for how he's been treating me, I would have planned a lovely birthday party for him. But now, why put forth any effort? He has not expressed any interest in seeing me today.

It's evening and I'm in my bedroom when I receive a call from Donna. "Are you coming up? We brought a cake for dad's birthday." How nice! He won't be alone. I feel a little sad but I am still protecting myself from the hurt Arthur has caused.

"Let me talk to your dad," I say. She puts Arthur on the phone.

"Donna asked if I am coming. Do you want me to come up?"

Arthur says, kindly, hopefully, "Yes, I'd really like it if you would come."

I pause, then agree. Although it's late and I am tired, I will suspend my reluctance to go out of my way for him because it's his birthday, because he asked. What a sucky way to spend a birthday – in rehab with a broken back. I make the hour's drive. In his bed, Arthur is mellow and weak. Donna lights the candles and we sing happy birthday to him. We pass a few pleasant hours together as we pretend that all is well.

The Week Before Mom Leaves

27

Francis has given me a drop-dead date of Friday for mom to leave my home and move into assisted living in the Lancaster area. Ten precious days together from that first call from Francis.

Mom continues to take the bus to her senior's group three times a week at the Medical Center and I continue to work.

Today, when I get home from work, mom is sitting in her chair by the window. My dad used to call this, "The face in the window." The lonely woman looking out. Watching. Waiting. Alone. I wonder if that's how mom feels?

Her TV tray sits in front of her, crossword puzzle and mail spread out. I walk over and sit down on the adjoining couch. "How was your day?" I ask.

"Okay."

"What did you talk about today in your workshop?"

"They asked some questions and some people in the circle answer their questions."

"What kind of questions?"

"Oh, you know, this and that."

She doesn't remember and asking her these questions will not provide answers. I want to connect with her, engage her, exercise her brain as she tries to recollect her day.

She shows me a paper given to her by the team at the hospital. It says, "Rose doesn't participate in the workshops. She is not engaged and when asked questions, she doesn't remember things." It ends with a reference to it not being a good fit. Her participation in this program may be short-lived. Interesting that it should come up this week, as we prepare to move her out. A confirmation that Mom isn't doing well.

On the nights I'm not visiting Arthur, Mom and I eat dinner together, savoring the last few evenings we have before she moves out. Tonight, we sit at the marble kitchen table looking out the window and watch the red Cardinals eating from the feeders. Conversation has stalled. We sit in silence. Then Mom says, "I don't know why I have to leave. Why do I have to leave?" My heart just broke.

What can I tell her? She is confused. Like me.

"I don't know, Mom." My throat is thick, clogged with sadness as I get up from my seat at the table and walk over to her and sit down in the chair next to her. "I wish you didn't have to go."

Mom opens her arms and I collapse in them. The pain of separating from my mom is unbearable. How many times do we say goodbye in a lifetime? At five-years old, I did not want to leave my mom to go to first grade. As an adult, I got married and moved to Maryland, leaving my family behind in Philadelphia. And twenty-eight years of goodbyes from her front porch after our weekend visits, watching her wave goodbye as we drove off. The last time I visited her, we hugged and I cried, "Mom, I can't keep doing this. It's too hard to leave you alone here."

But this one is final. She won't be coming back. This is the move of no return. Great racking sobs come from a place deep in my belly. She hugs me and I cling to her and we cry together, holding each other, grief pouring out like honey, thick and slow. Unbearably painful. There is nothing to say that will make it better. Nothing that will make this easier to understand or make this transition easier to abide. Not logic, "It's for the best," from well-meaning friends. Not encouragement from our neighbor Barbara to mom, "You'll love assisted living!" Nothing will remove the heartache, the wrenching of mom from her home or from me. The decision has been taken out of our hands and I am left to pick up my emotional pieces and mom's as well. The losses are too great to bear.

Afterwards, I go upstairs to her bedroom, stand in the threshold and look. Mom's bookcases overflow with first editions that she collected, Agatha Christie Mysteries that she loves, autobiographies of Lauren Bacall and Susan Boyle. Knick knacks scattered over bureaus and shelves collected over the years from friends. The large rosary from my father's casket hangs from a post on her brass bed.

I have to pack her up. *God, I don't know where to start.* This is too hard. *Why, God, why?* First my husband's accident, now my mother leaving. I can't fathom her leaving so soon.

I swing open the bi-fold closet door. Although we left many of her clothes in Philly, this closet is full. Here is the floral dress she bought last year when we were at Kmart. I doubt she'll wear it again. How dressed up will she need to be in her new facility?

Mom sits on her bed as I ask, "Do you like this? Do you wear this?" She says yes to everything. Brown pants and blue pants and beige pants. More than she'll need where she's going.

Then, watching me pack, she asks, "What are you doing?"

"I'm packing up your stuff."

"What for?"

"For you to move to assisted living."

Ice Cream With Mom

28

My last week with Mom. At work on Tuesday, my cell phone rings. It's one of the administrators from Mom's senior group. "I'm calling about Rose DiCicco. Is this her daughter?"

"Yes. What's going on?"

"Your Mom is fine," the caller says, "She fainted and we took her right away to the ER." Fortunately, her group meets in a hospital so she was easily transported to the ER.

I close my eyes. Breathe. *Oh God, please don't let this be serious*.

When I arrive at the hospital, Mom is in bed covered with white sheets, an intravenous line hooked up to her arm with a bag of fluid. Her face lights up, "Angela!"

I bend over to give her a kiss. "Hi Mom! How do you feel?"

I take her hand, pat her arm. It's wrinkled, her hands cold.

"I feel fine," she says, "I don't know why I'm here."

"They said you fainted. Do you remember anything?"

"No."

A few minutes later Mom turns to me and says, "I don't know why I'm here. Why am I here?"

We repeat this conversation several times, and then I take a piece of paper and pen out of my handbag. I write, "You are in the ER. You fainted. They are taking tests." I hand it to my mom, "Here Mom." She takes it in her right hand, reads it. Lays her hand down on the bed. A few minutes later, she picks up the paper and reads it again. I stand next to her bed and rub her arm. I sit down in the chair near her bed and wait.

Finally, the doctor comes in. Mom says, "This is my daughter Angela." She says it proudly. The doctor shakes my hand, then tells us the diagnosis. Mom has a urinary tract infection and is dehydrated.

"We see this in older patients. It's very common." The doctor explained that in elderly patients, UTI's and dehydration presents itself differently than in younger people. I wouldn't have recognized the symptoms. Mom wasn't in pain, but she was lethargic, unable to stay awake.

The diagnosis explains her recent behavior in her Senior Group, not participating, falling asleep during the sessions. I'm not surprised she is dehydrated. Water is anathema to mom. She drinks barely enough to take her pills and no amount of coaxing has altered her water intake. Water, she avoids at all costs. Wine, she can drink by the gallon.

Mom asks the doctor, "Can I go home?"

The doctor wants her to stay overnight for observation, "We want to make sure you're ok."

"But I want to go home."

"I know, but we don't want to send you home and then have

a problem."

Mom turns to me, "Angela, I want to go home. Please, please." Her voice is childlike, begging.

"I know, Mom, but the doctor thinks it's best if you stay."

Mom doesn't understand why she's here. She turns to the doctor, "Please let me go home. I don't want to stay here." She is like a child, begging not to be left behind, frightened to be in an unfamiliar place. I feel sad for her.

"Angela," she says in a stage whisper, "I don't want to stay here." She says it like we are conspirators, trying to find a way to break out of this place. I hold her hand. I offer reassurances. "I'll stay with you and go up to your room with you."

I'm tired and emotionally numb. Maybe God is showing me I can't handle two infirmed patients. Maybe this is a sign, a confirmation that Mom should be moved to a place where she can be monitored. Maybe.

In her hospital bed, she looks lost, my Mom of the BIG personality. I tell her, "I'll back tomorrow after work to take you home. I'll check up on you. You'll be okay." I tune the TV to the old black and white shows she enjoys watching. I kiss her goodbye on the cheek and leave.

If only Arthur was here to help her like he did before. But no, it can't be that way. Mom lost something too with Arthur's accident. It precipitated her moving into assisted living.

I have to let it go--Mom, her leaving, her feelings, her staying in the hospital. I have to let it all go for tonight.

When I arrive at the hospital the next day, Mom is sitting up and bright and perky. Her skin color is pink and healthy. Her eyes are clear. She is alert. Wow! I haven't seen her like this in a while.

Thursday evening

The night before mom leaves, I ask, "Mom, do you want to go get ice cream?"

Her face lights up and we drive to the ice cream shop. Mom's tastes are simple; she orders vanilla. My favorite is dark chocolate with peanut butter. We take our ice cream outside. I ask someone to take a photo of us and pose behind mom's chair. I keep the conversation light, soaking in the time we have together.

Inside, my heart is breaking. Our last evening together. We revisit memories of her time in Fort Belvoir when my dad was in the army. When her father, an Italian immigrant, visited them, there was only one bedroom. In his broken English, he said, "You hanga da sheet," gesturing between him and my mom and dad. Privacy.

Then mom says, "I prayed for life to be good and calm and happy and to be with my family."

Room for Rent

29

Survival. I feel as if I've been here before. Yes, I have, with my ex, figuring out how to pay the mortgage, keep the house, pay the bills with more money going out than coming in.

With Arthur's refusal to consider coming home after his rehab and with Mom leaving, I am panicked! I need to generate income quickly to replace the income lost from Mom's living expenses and Arthur's contribution to the mortgage. I place an ad on Craig's List. Craig's List is a site where you can meet people, find an apartment or join a band. My last two jobs were found on Craig's List (CL). Conveniently, you can also list a room for rent.

I post my ad and upload photos of the room: *Furnished*

*room for rent in lovely home on quiet street. Sunny bedroom
with windows and closet. Kitchen and laundry privileges.
Short-term rental. $650.*

Email responses start coming in. In my experience, men are typically less fussy about their lodging, and most of the woman I've rented to have not worked out. One left crusty dishes in her bedroom along with glasses and coffee mugs where unknown beverages bred mold. When she left, I had to fumigate the room. It was that disgusting.

One response stands out. He is looking for a short-term rental, which suits me perfectly. We set up an appointment for him to come over one evening.

When he arrives, I open the door to a stocky man with sandy hair. "Hi, I'm JJ!" he says with a smile as he thrusts his thick hand out to me. I like him instantly. A friend is with me so I feel comfortable letting him in the house. I take him upstairs and show him the room and the bath across the hall. "This is fine," JJ says standing in the doorway of the bedroom, "I only need a place to lay my head." We agree to the terms and he moves in the next day.

JJ turns out to be a God-send. An angel. I thank God every day for him and his willingness to help me around the house.

After working long days, he comes home looking beat. Yet he walks in the door and asks me, "What do you need me to do?" During the next few weeks JJ moves furniture and carries hundreds of boxes that need sorting. He paints one of the bedrooms and the hallway in exchange for a break on the rent.

While I am purging, I offer household goods and kitchen appliances to my kids so often they become irritated with me. Becca finally says in exasperation, "Mom! Stop asking me if I want things! I don't want your stuff!" I give a brand-new crock pot to JJ since I don't need two. Becca comes to regret her outburst when her crock pot cracks and she asks, "Do you have an extra?" No dear, you told me you didn't need anything.

Sometimes JJ brings his teenage son over to help. JJ told me, "My son thinks your 'touch' lamp is cool." We have so many lamps I am quite sure we could light up New York. I gift his son the touch lamp.

I gift JJ Christmas trees, decorations and the bedroom set my mom left. I don't know what I would do without his help making this terrible situation smoother than it might have been. Along with relief, I carry sadness with me, a weight on my shoulders; a catch in my throat.

I stand in the doorway of what was Mom's bedroom and see it as it was when we moved into the house fifteen years ago. Kevin, a high school senior, claimed the largest room, a privilege of the oldest child. I remember the bulletin board with photos on his wall, his baseball cards on the top shelves of the closet, his dress shirts hanging below.

Reminiscences swirl in my head as I stand there, sad to be leaving this home that holds many marvelous memories – weddings and baby showers and barbeques. Graduation parties, Christmas parties and holiday dinners. Sad that my children are grown and moved out. Sad that life moves on. And sad that we will not be making more memories here. My dream of leaving this house to my kids shattered.

Disneyworld has my favorite ride: The Haunted Mansion. As the car rides through the dining room, the table is filled with food and ghosts are feasting. In the ballroom ghosts are dancing. In the mirror, you'll see a ghost riding with you. That's what I see now. The ghost of Becca at age twelve in her room with her new captain's bed. Ghosts dancing on the deck at Ashley and Chris' wedding. Ghosts at Kevin's BBQ when he graduated from culinary school. I am haunted by ghosts from the past.

But the one that brings me to tears is the ghost at the bottom of the stairs.

Each day, when Arthur came home from work, he stood at the bottom of the stairs. I stood three steps up so we were face to face. I leaned into him and we shared a long kiss. It's on these stairs that I opened my heart and allowed myself to fall in love with Arthur.

Arthur Packs Up

30

Arthur calls me, a bit frantic, "You have a man renting already?"

"Yes, temporarily."

"All my stuff is in my office and it's valuable. I'm concerned about that." Not about me. Not about a strange man moving in and my safety. Not about my heart breaking because he says he's not coming home. But about his stuff.

"It would be nice if you were concerned about your wife more than your belongings."

"I am," he says belatedly, "But I have no control over that."

Every glimmer of hope for our relationship is snuffed out by these conversations.

Later, he calls and tells me, "Donna and her husband are

coming over tonight to pack up my stuff." Lord, give me strength.

Over several evenings, at Arthur's bequest, friends and family arrive to pack his belongings. They all have the same reaction, their eyes wide with disbelief as they stand in the doorway to his office or look in the basement. Piles of stuff greet them—books from college, furniture, tools, CD's he never listened to, a TV that was never hooked up. Much of it should be trashed or donated. Do I pack every last paper clip or weed through it? Why waste energy on items he may never use again? He hasn't yet come to that realization. He has a $200 Inversion Table designed to help with back pain that did nothing but take up space in our family room. Sailboat supplies? He won't be sailing his boat again. Camping gear? In the years we've been together, he's never wanted to take me camping, though I asked him many times.

I had romantic notions of looking at the stars together, of snuggling together in our tent. People are always surprised to hear that I enjoy camping because I'm a girly-girl, pink ruffles and sparkly tiaras, squeamish about bugs and snakes, but I love camping. I camped with my kids every summer when they were growing up. I know how to pitch a tent.

"Too much work," Arthur said, remembering setting up camp alone with two small children.

"But I'll help you," I said, "You won't be doing it alone!" He steadfastly refused. The camping gear that he wants packed up mocks me.

Over several days of packing, all the empty space in the living room is piled high with his boxes, labeled shirts, shoes, boat supplies.

On Wednesday, the movers arrive early to take Arthur's stuff to Baltimore. The neighbor Rita is recruited by Arthur to meet the movers at the storage unit. I asked the movers to keep the shelves intact to use them in the storage unit. Instead, they haphazardly piled everything up. As a result, Rita authorizes a third storage unit in her name. Another boundary issue.

When the movers leave, I grieve. I grieve for Arthur, the accident, our marriage. I grieve for the house and the life I created here. Remembering our family's first Thanksgiving here, the table set with Lenox China on gold chargers, matching napkins and gold flatware, crystal glasses. I remember the joy of finally having a family room large enough to have Super Bowl parties and movie nights with friends. These and so many more memories waft and tug at me. *Is it the end of us too?*

After Arthur moved in to the house, he began changing things, making the house his own, but without including me. He moved the cat litter from the laundry room into the breakfast room, worried they would pee on his clothes. He moved my conveniently placed batteries and light bulbs from the hall closet inconveniently into the basement. One incident in particular stands out because it represented my independence. During my single years, I created a path of large oval stones from the driveway to the yard. I noticed Arthur had dug them up and rearranged them. *Why?* Why would you do that without conferring with me? It's no small thing, those stones that I bought myself, carefully measured and placed.

Ironically, it is those memories that give me the impetus to continue this journey of living separately.

Yes, I Can Sing

31

September 2015

My life is no fun at all. I work and then drive an hour to visit Arthur. I pack before work, late at night and anytime in between. I have nothing to look forward to. I used to say, "My middle name is 'fun.' If it's not fun, I'm not doing it!" I sought out enjoyable jobs and spiced up daily life. Why do it if it's not fun?

When the kids were small, we celebrated everything! Cinco de Mayo dinner with colorful placemats and tacos. Pancakes for dinner on National Upside-Down Day. Red, white and blue crepe paper and sparkly stars on their bikes and wagons for the 4th of July parade.

I made learning fun too. When my seven-year-old son was learning the States and Capitals, I helped him remember North and South Dakota. South Dakota's capital is Pierre. South Dakota is peeing in the air to North Dakota. To this day my kids remember that!

Now, my life is serious, with nearly every hour eaten up with things to DO. No time for fun or adventures. What to pack, what to sell. Visit Arthur, talk to the doctors. I'm living one minute at a time, utterly exhausted. Sometimes, when I visit Arthur, I am so exhausted that I climb in the hospital bed with him. Snug in his arms, we are joined as one. In his arms, I forget all the angst, all the pain. Ironically, in his arms, I feel safe.

In the middle of this crisis which knows no end, I need an outlet and decide I need to sing. I love to sing but it's been years since I enjoyed it. In the 70's, I was in a band where I met my first husband. In grade school I sang soprano in the choir and alto in the guitar group at my church.

I check out Craig's List for bands seeking a female singer, preferably one that isn't too intense. My life is too busy for big commitments. This is for fun.

I find an ad and respond to it: *I'm in my 50's, love to sing. Many moons ago I was in a band that did covers. I can sing alto and love doing harmony. My natural range is similar to Carole King's.*

I quickly receive a response and we agree to meet on Saturday. I listen to Carole King's *Tapestry* album. I sing in my car to Janis Ian's *At Seventeen* album. My voice is good, perhaps the best it's ever been. I have nothing to lose. Nothing. What can I lose after I have already lost so much?

When the audition rolls around, I am excited. This is my secret. No one knows that I am trying out for a band. In fact, many of my friends don't know I was ever IN a band, let alone sing. I take my music stand and a bottle of water with me. The singer travels light. The drummer has the heaviest load so practice is typically at the drummer's house. Surprisingly, I am not nervous for the audition. In fact, I rock it singing *Up on the Roof* and a few other songs. They like me!

I'm in a band! For a few hours every other Saturday, I am free, thinking of nothing but the music. No one here knows my story. They don't know Arthur or about the accident. They don't know I am selling my house and I don't know where I'm moving to. For one afternoon, my life is beautiful, my voice lifts in song. They know nothing and this is bliss.

House For Sale

32

Without much time or energy to shop for realtors, when a friend recommends one, I agree to meet with her. Sitting at my kitchen table, after showing me massive amounts of credentials, I sign her on. Shortly, my house will be on the market. The realtor and her husband are a team. She works on selling the house and all the details. He is a handyman and at ten dollars an hour, he's a bargain.

Several years ago, Arthur and I pulled up the original tiles on the family room floor with the intention to replace them. Arthur and I couldn't agree on the flooring. The floor remained bare. And now it has to be finished to sell the house.

I go to Home Depot with my friend Jim to pick out laminate

flooring. I hire Steve to lay it in the family room. Steve also adds fresh white paint to my porch railing for curb appeal. He fixes the bi-fold doors in Arthur's office that were perpetually off track. My experience with selling a house, and this is the fourth house I'm selling, is that we fix it up so the next tenant can enjoy it. My last house badly needed the hardwood floors refinished. With three kids and a mortgage, I couldn't prioritize it. But I had the floors refinished before I put the house up for sale. Why do we do that? Wait to fix up our space, as if we don't deserve it?

I'm panicked with too much to do and too little time to do it. The house needs windows washed, floors mopped and furniture moved to be ready to stage and have photos taken for the listing. I'm relying on the timetable of others and I'll take whatever they offer- JJ, Steve, my son-in-law Chris. The clock is ticking and I'm afraid, so afraid I'm making a mistake selling the house, even while it overwhelms me to keep it up and to get it ready to list. I email my friends again to ask for help and we plan another workday on Sunday.

In the meantime, my mind refuses to cooperate; it's tired of making decisions: Do I keep my mom's first edition books? If I keep them, what will I do with them? *Do I need ten sets of sheets?* My back aches from weeding the garden with a friend last evening. A migraine has been threatening for four days.

On Sunday, nine friends show up. Relieved, I send up a prayer, *Thank you God for sending friends to help.* I can see His hand in these little things.

When they leave, I look around, grateful for all the work they did. Then I realize this neat, clean and uncluttered house is no longer a home; it's a shell, void of personal items and family photographs. It's void of ME, my personality and energy.

Later, as I lie in bed, I try to remember what it was like when Arthur was here. When he slept on the pillow beside me. When he made my morning coffee. The house is also void of Arthur.

The next day, the photographer comes. It's real now. The process is in motion.

Within two weeks, the house is sold. I have a deadline, an ending to this chapter in my life. This place. This home. My place. My home.

When a friend of mine was selling her house, she told me, "I acted like it was someone else's house." If I imagine the house as no longer my own, but as someone else's, it's easier to continue clearing out. It puts a layer of objectivity between me and the home.

Arthur is now lucid; the drugs that were wreaking havoc with his thinking are out of his system. He helps pay the mortgage. He sees the wreckage of his choices. We have an honest conversation. "I wish I hadn't bailed on the house," he tells me. He's scared, I'm scared. Our future is uncertain.

I pray: *Lord, you brought me to this home and you'll bring me to the next home, one that is perfect for the next phase of my life, filled with family and friends. A lovely home more suited for my future and, God willing, Arthur's. I put our situation in your hands. I trust that we will come out of this better, stronger as a couple, even as I move along with uncertainty. You are certain and I'll rest in that.*

When I come downstairs in the morning, sunlight is splayed across the hardwood floor. The living room, nearly empty, is peaceful but it doesn't look lived in. The plants thrive in the bay window. *Will there be a place for my plants wherever I move to?*

As I sit with my morning coffee, sad about leaving the house and not decorating for the holidays, tears spill down my face. *What about our annual Pumpkin Carving?* Begun when the kids were little, it filled in the space where my nuclear family in Philadelphia used to be since we couldn't visit each other anymore on Halloween. While my kids carved out simple faces, scooping out the pumpkin seeds which I would roast, I'd read an Edgar Allan Poem, *Annabel Lee* or *The Raven*

As the kids grew, so did the event as we added friends and then spouses. Now there is a new litter of kids to share this tradition with - my grandkids in their cute costumes, witches, princesses, superheroes. I didn't know that last year would be my last Pumpkin Carving or Thanksgiving or the last anything.

Deeply sad, I cry on the phone to Becca, "I wanted one last Pumpkin Carving!"

"Mom," she says so kindly, "I don't think one more pumpkin carving will fill the hole you have in your heart." She's right. Nothing can fill this gaping hole. Things are happening lightning quick.

Three months ago, I had a full life, a full house. Mom and our cats lived with us. We were packing for vacation. Now, mom moved out, Arthur won't come home, our cat Denim is gone, a renter is in and the house is being sold.

Friends remind me I will build new memories. And the old ones remain. It is not enough.

I thought my kids would get the house. I thought I would live here until I died and my house would be passed on to my kids. It would stay in the family, this lovely five-bedroom home. My grandkids would play in the yard. I would continue to host Christmas Eve dinner.

In 2000, when I moved in, I stood on the landing of the stairs, looked down into the expansive living room and felt gratitude. Space! I was finally able to spread out after too many cramped years in a small house. My gratitude never went away. I would continue to stand on the upper landing looking down, grateful, every single time.

Now I am concerned about feeling cramped again in my next home.

Change. The only constant in life. Will Arthur and I be together?

I ask God to help me get through this. *Do I stay with him, Lord? What should I do?* My brother says, "God isn't going to tell you to leave him."

Now what, Oh Lord, now what?

It's Tuesday. I'm terrified. I wake up frightened every day, fear lodged in my chest, burning in my belly. *What am I DOING?* I imagine staying here, keeping the house myself, undoing the sale. *It's not too late, is it?* I'm scared because I don't know where I'm going to live. I'm scared to live with Arthur. I don't know how to live with someone in a wheelchair. I'm scared I won't like living in a condo or bedroom or apartment. I'm scared that I don't love him anymore. I didn't want to kiss him when I left the other night.

Why do I continue to go visit Arthur? I am playacting. I feel nothing or close to it. I understand couple's go through this. Maybe it's a season. This I know: No matter how many times I walk away, I hear God's voice, *"Go back."* I hear, *"Stay, it will be better on the other side."*

There's freedom in being away from Arthur. Freedom to join a band. I have more energy, not being drained by Arthur. I've built an emotional wall, not letting him get too close to hurt me. *Can he change? Should we stay separated until our issues are worked out?* It will be harder to leave if we live together. I'm afraid of being trapped, of not being attracted to him anymore.

I heard a slogan that I adopt: *When you don't know what to do, do nothing.* For now, I do nothing.

On Friday I visit Arthur. He has a grey beard now. It's easier for him than shaving daily. His bald head now has a monk's halo of grey. He looks old and not like the man I know. He tells me he loves me. I say, "I'm still here and I love you."

I'm still scared.

Nowhere to Go

33

Wednesday, October 21, 2015

Arthur's insurance coverage at rehab ends on Monday. "Maybe I can still come home," he says, hopefully.

"That ship has sailed," I tell him. His eyes are downcast, he looks so sad. He knows his actions contributed to the decision to sell the house. *What would have happened if I rode it out? If I stayed through the chaos?* It doesn't matter, the what-ifs. It's too late. Don't look back.

The paperwork for the assisted living he is to be transferred to has been completed. I see a light at the end of this tunnel, an end in sight to the long road traveling to visit Arthur, to the late nights driving home, because he'll be closer now. I found a place near my job, easy enough to skip over to after work.

I pull in to the parking lot at work and my phone rings. It's Don from the assisted living. The morning call sets the tone for the next few days.

"I have bad news." Pause. "They won't accept Arthur."

"What???" My head exploded. "What do you mean they won't accept him? They already accepted him! I put in all the paperwork!" In a tizzy, I am grasping. "I don't understand how they can back out after we applied and they accepted. How can they do this?" Don doesn't have any answers. "See if you can talk to them, get them to reconsider."

"I'll see what I can do."

I thought this transition was going smoothly. A quick prayer, *God, what is going on?! I can't take anymore!* I go into the office and sit at my desk. I want to cry. Or scream. Or both. I call Don several times throughout the day and he doesn't pick up. I leave messages, "Please call me." And "I need to know what's going on."

I call Arthur, "What are we going to do?" I hope Arthur has an answer, a suggestion, a solution. We notify his social worker. She explains that if we don't find a facility for Arthur by Sunday, he has two choices: He will be released to a nursing home where he pays out of pocket or he can pay $14,500 in advance to stay at his current rehab for thirty days.

I sit in my car after work and call Don again. He finally picks up. "What did you find out?" Nothing. I drive home and walk into the empty house. *What do I need to do now?* I call the assisted living again and ask to speak to someone about the decision made about Arthur. I am surprised when the head nurse comes on the phone.

"Hi! I don't understand the decision to not accept Arthur."

"We made the decision after reading his chart," she says. *Didn't they read his chart before they accepted Arthur?* "It was decided that he is high-needs and the facility already has three high-needs patients. The staff would be stretched too thin." *Why did they wait to make this decision? Don't they realize how it impacts our lives?* The director recommends a few other places for Arthur. I sink my head in my hands, cover my eyes, crushed, deflated. Out of options.

On Thursday morning I call one of the recommended facilities. A nurse is immediately sent to Arthur for an evaluation. Each facility needs to do its own evaluation. By the time I call Arthur, he has already been contacted. He says, "The Wound Specialist is on her way down to have a pressure sore looked at." After examining Arthur's pressure sore, she bumps the wound up to a Stage 3 – involves deeper layers of skin.

This is NOT good news. Arthur is turned down again. With a Stage 3 pressure sore, no assisted living facility in the state of Maryland can legally take him. That leaves long term care facilities i.e., nursing homes. Arthur doesn't belong in a nursing home! At my desk, I try to keep my head on my job while furiously trying to figure out what to do for Arthur. I need to find him a place to stay. And get the wound downgraded to a Stage 2.

I call Arthur again, "You must have your wound looked at on Friday and have it downgraded to a two again." His next step depends on the pressure sore being downgraded. Everything, Arthur's immediate future, the financial impact, everything depends on this diagnosis. "Make yourself REAL to them, make yourself a person! You're not a number, a patient, you're a person!"

This time, the Wound Specialist says, "Maybe the covering was old lotion." She downgrades the wound to a two. All that stress for nothing!

In the meantime, I find two possible places for Arthur. After work on Thursday, I drive to one of them, a home turned into an assisted living. On the way, I berate myself for not visiting these facilities sooner. *Why did I not have a back-up plan in place?*

As I pull into the driveway, my heart sinks. The grass is over-grown, the siding needs washing and the windows are grimy. This is not a place I would normally entertain for Arthur, but I am desperate.

An aide answers the door, then takes me on a tour. It's a small house, not well kept up. Worn rugs and drab walls that need painting. An odor, like stale cigarettes, lingers. A white-haired woman wanders aimlessly, in some phase of dementia. Another woman stares at the ceiling from her bed, mouth agape like my Aunt Alice the last time I saw her. My heart races. A narrow, dingy hall takes us to the room Arthur would occupy next to a small bathroom with a dated sink and missing knobs on the cabinet. *Could he get his wheelchair in here?* The shower has cleanser sprinkled on it. "Is the shower cleaned after each use?" I ask.

The aide nods her head and says, "Yes," but I am doubtful; alarms are going off in my head. My stomach rolls. I have to get out of here. I want to run. I do not want Arthur to stay here, in this gloom.

I exit quickly back to my car, shutting the door behind me. Shutting out the shabby house, but the grimy feeling clings to me. I reach for my keys and can't find them! My internal chaos is showing up outwardly. I empty my purse on the front seat; not there. I rush back to the house to ask about my keys then run back to the car. I look around frantic, not on the ground; not in the car. I worry about being late for my appointment at the next facility. One last look and there, slipped between the door and the seat, are my keys. I sigh, relieved. I call my next appointment and tell the owner, "I'm on my way!"

A short while later, I pull into a beautiful development and drive up to a stately home. *Is this it?*

I knock on the solid oak door. Karen, the owner answers

and invites me in. Stepping into the foyer is like walking into Heaven. It's large and grand, ceramic tiles and a gold chandelier with crystals. I am shown the kitchen with granite countertops. The deck, large enough for Arthur to wheel himself around, the sun beginning to set. *What a magnificent view!* This place is beautiful! It would be wonderful for Arthur! I am afraid to ask the question, afraid to hear the answer. "Can you take us?" Karen says she needs to see Arthur and evaluate him, but not until Saturday. Two days from now. My shoulders sag. That's cutting it too close for the Sunday deadline.

Karen sees my angst and asks, "Would you feel better if I could get up there Friday afternoon?"

"Yes!" *Yes, I would!* Much better. Breathe Angela. Breathe.

As I leave, Karen gives me a comforting hug and tells me not to worry about anything. I want to be reassured. I want to not worry. But with all the roadblocks this week, I won't feel secure until Arthur is settled in his new place.

Why, God, when I have prayed and done what I thought you wanted me to do, are you throwing me this curve ball at the eleventh hour? Was there a clue, some intuition that I missed?

On Friday, Karen meets with Arthur. Arthur said the visit went well, however, that's what we thought with the others. Pins and needles.

I try to let it go, turn it over to God, look for the blessings, the peace, the serenity.

It's Saturday morning. My grandson's second birthday party is later today – something to look forward to. But first I need to drop off Arthur's paperwork to Karen. "How did the visit with Arthur go?" I ask when I arrive at her house.

"Everything is fine," Karen says.

"You're going to take Arthur?"

"Yes," she says. Relief floods my body.

Please, God, NO MORE ROADBLOCKS.

Finally, I can stop thinking about Arthur and enjoy my grandson's birthday!

Before I left this morning with no card, no gift and no time, I grabbed some children's books, tossed them in a blue bag with tissue paper and ran out the door. I knew he wouldn't know the difference; I knew my daughter wouldn't mind.

My grandson greets me at the door, reaches for the little gift bag, pulls out one of the chunky board books, and sits on the floor flipping through the pages. In those few moments, all is well.

Leaving Rehab

34

Sunday, October 25, 2015

I stay up late writing to get it all down on paper. All the details that would later be forgotten. When I am finally in bed at 1:00 a.m., I can't sleep. I toss and I turn; I process my life. I worry. At 2:00 a.m. I get out of bed and do what I do when I can't sleep: I eat! I fall into bed at 3:00 a.m.; I will have only five hours of sleep. Fortunately, I took Monday off to help Arthur transition from his current rehab to his new home in Olney, MD.

Monday, October 26, 2015

I wake up at 8:00 a.m. wondering how the day will go, worried about the bottom falling out, as it did with the last assisted living. Spin, spin, spin. My head spins. *Will it all fall into place?*

Papers signed? Calls made to the social worker?

At 10:00 a.m. I leave the house. I stop to get gas before my tank runs dry, leaving an hour to drive to the rehab and less than an hour to pack Arthur's things up. Arthur's belongings need to be cleared out of his room by noon. When I arrive at rehab, Arthur is still in bed. I begin packing up his personal items, CD player, books, lamps, and make my first trip out to the car. After three trips, my husband says, "They have dollies here." *NOW you tell me?*

When I'm finished, my legs feel like spaghetti, my exhaustion already high. We sit, waiting for the release papers to be signed by his doctor. Finally, the papers are delivered to us in the waiting area. Arthur takes another step toward freedom.

I drive the car around to the rehab center where Arthur is waiting. Two therapists are ready to help Arthur into the car. I watch and learn, since I'll be the one helping him going forward.

It is sad looking at those legs that won't work, that would likely never work, as Arthur slides on a board from the wheelchair to the car seat. Arthur used to drive when we went out. Now, he is a passenger and I am driving. So many changes, large and small.

This is Arthur's first taste of freedom since the accident. He has not seen or done anything normal since June. Four months ago. I hope he can appreciate the gorgeous fall colors, the leaves on the trees.

He isn't hungry, although I am. I had a fantasy of going into a restaurant like we did before the accident; unfortunately, it's too soon. Getting in and out of the car is a process and we need two people to do it. A drive-thru is the best we can do. We pull into McDonald's. I ask Arthur what he wants. "A milkshake! I haven't had one in a long time." His first taste of normal. After getting our order, we pull into a shady spot in the parking lot and pretend we are having a picnic lunch.

As we continue our drive, Arthur is quiet. "What are you thinking?" I ask.

"I'm looking at the trees changing color," he says, "I'm taking it all in."

Back in Rockville, I drop off his prescriptions to the pharmacy, doing what Arthur can't yet do for himself. When I return to the car, I ask, "Do you want to ride back home to see our house?" He agrees and I take him to our home. Driving through the neighborhood with him, I wish I was taking him home for good; that none of this had happened and this was a typical day. He would walk through the front door and into the house and we could resume our lives.

Arthur is re-familiarizing himself with sights he hasn't seen in months. When he left our house the evening of June 11, neither of us knew our lives would be changed. We were simply and blissfully looking forward to our trip to Chincoteaque to celebrate our fifth wedding anniversary.

As I pull into our driveway and park, my tears begin to flow. Looking around I am reminded of all the things Arthur had done outside- mow the lawn, pull up weeds, wash windows. And all the things he did inside, ceiling fans and lights in my closet and painting the bathroom vanity. He won't get to do any of those things again.

"I'm sad too," Arthur says.

As far as I know, he hasn't shed a single tear. After the drugs were flushed out of his system, we talked about processing the grief. I know we have not finished this process. We have barely scratched the surface because we are still in the thick of it. I told him it was okay to cry. That he needed to cry. God knows I've cried buckets of tears.

He said he had been trained not to cry. As a child, his father would discipline him with a belt. If he cried too soon, the beating continued; if he didn't cry soon enough, the beating continued. He learned to manage his feelings. He told me earlier he wasn't comfortable crying in the rehab, didn't feel safe with all the people coming and going in his room. Maybe once he starts, when he finally feels safe with a room of his own, he will wail and gnash his teeth and cry for hours or days.

Arthur is thirsty and asks for water. As I step into the house, I no longer feel Arthur's presence. I imagine he could have wheeled around the first floor. At least for a while, it would have been okay. At least part of my life would have been the same.

We pull out of the driveway and head to Arthur's temporary home, just ten minutes away. I watch his reaction as we drive up because the house is stately, beautiful. Arthur isn't one for grandiose words. He gives an understated, "It's nice." Karen has been expecting us and comes out with a Certified Nursing Assistant and we begin transferring Arthur from the car to his wheelchair. They need guidance and Arthur does an admirable job of communicating each direction. They wheel him up the ramp and I give him a quick tour of the house, his room, the bathroom next to his room, the one too small for his wheelchair. The one he will never use. He seems satisfied, especially with the expansive view from the kitchen.

I am wiped out. "I'll come back tonight," I tell Arthur.

After picking up his prescriptions, I go home, crawl into bed, exhaustion deep in my bones. Weariness.

My nap is over too soon. I get up, grab a bite to eat, then head back over to Arthur's place. He's been in his wheelchair most of the day and he looks exhausted. His head hangs, lines ring his eyes, his spirit seems broken. We watch TV together, my hand on his leg. Then I realize he can't feel it.

My husband can't feel his legs. Over and over again I process this information. I cry at the sight of these beautiful legs, unable to work. These strong muscular legs that ran, biked, buzzing constantly, now at rest. His muscles have gone limp, he lacks tone. *What can I do to keep his legs from atrophying?* I start tapping on them, hoping, hoping a connection will be made, that a holistic approach will bear fruit.

It's time to leave. I give thanks to God that my drive is only ten minutes instead of one hour.

Once home, I walk out onto my deck. I enjoy looking up at the stars at the end of the day. Tonight, I sit on my chair and look at the empty space where the gazebo was. The buyers didn't want it so it was removed today. My husband accurately described it as my sanctuary. Under its cover, I could have shade during the day to enjoy my coffee or entertain friends. In the rain, I could sit and listen, enjoying the sounds while staying dry.

Now, the space stands empty, as it was when I purchased the house. The wind blows, rustling the leaves in the trees. With the gazebo gone I feel unprotected, yet, to my surprise, I am enjoying the unobstructed view.

The house is sold, Arthur is settled in his new digs. Now I need to focus on me.

Friends ask, "Where are you moving to?"

"I have no idea!" I tell them.

"You've sold your house and you don't know where you're going?"

Correct. This is a huge leap of faith.

Definition of Faith (noun): complete trust or confidence in someone or something.

I don't trust myself, however, I do trust God. I don't have the whole picture; I know He does. I know He has my best interests in mind and however this turns out, it will be okay. I will be okay.

Sort, Toss, Give Away

35

Thursday, October 29, 2015

I live a lifetime before getting to work at 10:00 a.m. Before my eyes open, my foggy mind questions what day it is. Do I have to go to work? What's on today's agenda? The minute I open my eyes, my mind is racing. *Did it ever stop racing during the night?* I wake up exhausted rather than refreshed.

I groggily pad downstairs in my pj's and make the coffee. One morning I was so tired I added fresh coffee to the grinds leftover from the previous day. Another morning I turned the pot on without adding water. *Why is the coffee pot making that strange noise?* I stare at the pot, expecting it to tell me what the problem is. It takes a few moments before it dawns on me and I quickly add water to the pot. I miss Arthur making coffee the night before and setting the timer so it's brewing when I come into the kitchen.

While the coffee brews, I put in a load of laundry and make my lunch – a quick provolone and ham sandwich. Then I clear out a few kitchen drawers-- old kitchen towels (toss), wicker trivets (give away). I pack a few boxes and make a list for my upcoming estate sale:

1.Craft area: ribbon, lace, buttons, brooches. *What can I let go of?*

2.Towels, clothes, dishes: *How many sets of dishes do I need?*

3.Furniture: keep or sell the corner pine cabinet that smells deliciously like the scented candles I stored in there?

When my coffee is finished, I pour the steaming coffee into the blue pottery mug, grab milk, splash it in my coffee. If I change my routine, I may put milk in the coffee pot or my mug in the refrigerator.

The steaming hot coffee is warm and soothing in my hands. This is my favorite part of the day. I breathe IN the morning, the day, the coffee. I breathe. I sit. I listen to the quiet. Did you know you can hear quiet?

I close my eyes to meditate, to pray. My body feels heavy under the weight of responsibility and pressure of time, as a long to-do list cascades in my head.

Lord, tell me what to keep and what to let go of. Give me the strength to get through these next few weeks before the settlement on November 24. Help me to let go of this house that has been such a haven for me all these years. My heart is breaking, Lord and I'm tired. Bone tired.

Meditation time is up and I'm on the clock. I quickly eat my oatmeal then shower, dress, and dash off to work.

It's a slow day at work, and with so much to do at home I am vibrating with tension.

Once home, I eat a quick dinner then decide to spend time

in the utility/tool room, an overwhelming task. Where does one begin? So many crowbars, hammers, and saws - hacksaws, bow saws, jig saws. Six electric circular saws. Who needs this many? Answer: no one. It's a part of the disease Arthur had. The disease to accumulate, to have more, to stockpile. Did it make him feel safe? It was all an illusion.

When it became clear Arthur wasn't coming back, I called my son, "Kevin, when can you come over to go through the tools?" It's a big ask. Generations of tools are stored in the basement, from my grandfather and my dad to Arthur's collection of tools.

Kevin came over and spent an afternoon amongst the chaos, picking through Arthur's many toolboxes searching for tools that belonged to my dad (etched with P.A.D.) or my grandfather. He later told me, "I stood there looking around and was so overwhelmed, I had to go out on the deck for a half hour before I could face it again."

In 1997, when Kevin was twelve years old, my dad passed away from Myasthenia Gravis, an autoimmune neuromuscular disorder that affects the voluntary muscles. He lost the ability to work with his hands. His beautiful, strong, capable hands that could fix anything, make anything.

When my kids were little, my parents would make the three-hour drive from Philadelphia to visit us. They'd arrive at 8:00 a.m. Saturday morning and my kids would rush to the door to greet them, jumping up and down and hugging. Then my dad would go out to the car to bring in the suitcases. Each time he came, he carried a black hard case filled with tools into the house and asked, "What needs to be done around here?"

While cleaning out the basement, Kevin found that black case, completely intact. "Mom, I just lost it," he later told me. I imagine my grown son sobbing with grief. I wish I had been there to hold him.

When I visit Arthur at rehab and tell him what still needs to be done, he says, "I feel badly I didn't go through my stuff." He has reached the realistic conclusion that he won't be able to use most of it and he should have let me sell it. He slumps in his chair, his head dips down. I ask him if he is sad because he couldn't do these things any more – bike riding, mowing, fixing things around the house.

"No," he says, "I'm sad because I didn't need all of this stuff and I should have gone through it. I've left a big mess." He's quiet for a moment. "I don't know why I ever thought I needed a man cave. I don't like being alone and it's dark down there."

So much accumulation. So much weight.

After my divorce, I asked my three children to come over one Saturday. We emptied the entire attic. Building blocks, Beanie Babies and Barbies. Clothes that were special—a sweatshirt signed by classmates, a Tweety Bird shirt that Becca loved.

Massive amounts of stuff were donated and the rest was stored in the attic again. A huge weight had been lifted. The house felt lighter, I felt lighter. The physical weight of the attic was weighing me down and I didn't know it.

The weight of Arthur's stuff was weighing him down too. He didn't know it.

So much stuff - stuffed things, stuffed emotions. Could the term "back-breaking" be used literally here?

Moving Day Draws Near

36

The day of moving out draws closer. I need more time. More time in the house, more time to say goodbye. More time to let go.

I touch the white enamel towel rack Arthur installed in our bathroom, feeling sad. Saying goodbye to the familiar, to the little touches one adds to a house to make it their own.

This can't be happening in three weeks. In THREE WEEKS, I have to leave my beautiful home, my dream home. My life. Leave my life behind. My dismantled life. When I say this to my good friend Connie, she replies, "Yes, and what was dismantled you can put back together." Connie understands about being uprooted and rebuilding. She has been through her own transitions.

For the first time in thirty-five years, I won't own a home. I'm sad. I'm scared.

I didn't know last year would be the last Thanksgiving, the last Christmas, in my beautiful home. I didn't know I wouldn't have any more pumpkin carvings here. Where will I decorate?

Oh! I just remember that I haven't even been in the attic yet! One more thing to add to the already overwhelming list:

- Pick a storage place and a date to move my stuff into storage.
- Find a place to live.
- Get in the attic. Ugh.
- Go through stuff from the attic. Ugh.
- Hall closet. My closet. Foyer closet.

My list continues. When do you take down a computer you use every day? Moving day? The day before moving day?

It would be best if I had a place to move INTO before I must leave here. Will I need a bed and bureau or will it be furnished?

Ugh again.

The more I do, the more I see what needs to be done.

I'll miss odd things, like my top-down-bottom-up shades, a splurge after the divorce. They represent my independence. And the ceiling fan Arthur installed in our bedroom with a remote? Luxury. The lights Arthur put in my closet as a surprise one weekend when I was away. Sweet little touches.

Goodbye bedroom, my haven, good bye top-down bottom-up blinds, goodbye large lovely house with five bedrooms I have been so proud to own.

It's overwhelming. The grief is crushing.

Three weeks. That's it. Three. Weeks. It can't be happening. It can't be true.

It is.

For the last several years, as the upkeep on my home became a drain on both finances and energy, I've said I'm not sure

I want to own a home again. I could live in a box and be happy! Now I realize that was a fantasy. I don't want to live in a box! I want a home! I enjoy nesting, changing curtains each season and decorating for each holiday. Owning a home, I feel rooted. I feel rich.

I'll get through this. The crisis. the sale of the house. My marriage. And on the other side will be a wonderful new life. A fresh life. A simpler life. An uncomplicated life. I hope.

I'm not going to resolve anything tonight. Best to go to bed. I turn out the light, close my eyes and pray.

Each Day a Little Different

37

Friday–Monday
October 30–November 2, 2015

Having a moving sale is not how I want to spend Halloween. Fall is such a cozy time and my home is usually filled with straw bales, cobwebs and spooky music. In the bay window, I create a spooky Halloween Village of music boxes and dancing figurines collected over the years. When turned on, witches fly, ghosts howl and crystal balls are read. Where will I decorate now? Is the season of decorating my house for every holiday over already? I have grandchildren to share my story with!

After the sale, I will try to squeeze in seeing my grandkids in their Halloween costumes and then go dancing with friends. It promises to be a very long day indeed.

My friend Alan helps me prepare for tomorrow's moving sale. We don't see each other frequently, yet Alan remembers me in the summer and leaves zucchinis and tomatoes on the porch from his garden. Alan has a green thumb. And a soft heart. His hanging plants leave me breathless, so full and lush, spilling over the sides in a cacophony of color. He rescues dogs and people. When he offered help yesterday, I said, "No, I'm good." Why did I think I could do this alone? I'll need lots of help! I'm glad I reconsidered and Alan is available.

Late Friday evening, I flop into bed exhausted. I pray, *God, I need to wake up at 7:00 a.m.* Alarms are too alarming for me. They jar my system. God is my timer and my prayer rarely fails.

Morning rolls around. I groggily open an eye and look at the clock on my nightstand. 7:00 a.m. It's not happening. My heavy eyelids win the battle and I close my eyes again until 8:00 a.m. Then I do something I never do: I get out of bed and get dressed! This is my mother's habit, not mine. When Mom put her feet on the floor, she was dressed and ready for the day. I loll around in my pajamas as long as possible.

When Alan arrives, he hands me a brown bag with a gift inside: an Egg McGriddle! I love McGriddles! They have syrup in the muffin so it's sweet and salty. His thoughtfulness touches me. Now I don't have to worry about breakfast.

Alan and I head down to the basement where multiple circular saws, hand saws and more screwdrivers, nails and hammers than any one person could use in a lifetime are ready for sale. I suddenly see Kevin building the work stand in the utility room, tools hanging from the pegboard above, when we thought he would stay here, eventually buying the house. Although Kevin and I both went through the tools, I spy a hammer that was my dad's, a level, a tape measure with his initials on it. I take these and go back upstairs, focusing on the next task. There is no time to be sad, no time to grieve or cry or change my mind about selling the house. The wheels are in motion. I am swept up in the tide of momentum.

I glance at my phone and see a text from Arthur asking for passwords. He wants them now. NOW. *Why would he need passwords?* My shoulders slump, the burden of one more thing in the middle of the sale. I am tired and have no patience for him and his needs. I send a quick text, "I can't deal with this right now."

He sends back a text, "Can you please be nicer to me when I'm trying to help?" *Help how?*

The sale is over by 1:00 p.m. I look around the living room and dining room; The sale didn't make a dent. Both are still completely full.

I go upstairs and take a nap. Then I get up and get dressed in my Halloween costume – my annual Goth attire, black lipstick and nail polish.

Have I mentioned that Halloween is one of my favorite holidays? I refuse to let Halloween go by without doing something fun! Around 6:00 p.m., I meet up with my daughter Ashley's family. They look adorable as both kids and parents are dressed as Scooby Doo characters. I snap some pictures, then leave to meet friends at a Halloween dance. What a fun night off with friends! Away from thoughts, yard sales and the impending sale of my house.

When I come home, I glance around the living room seeing all the items that didn't sell. So many decisions, large and small and unimportant like what do I do with all of this yarn? I quickly run upstairs and get into my soft, cozy pajamas.

Monday, November 2, 2015

Every day is a little different. I plan one thing and another takes its place. Inching toward the November 23 settlement on the house, I wake up scared again. Since it has sold, I'm scared I'll regret not keeping it, scared of the future, scared that I have no place to live.

After work, I plan to go home, rest and pack more boxes. After dinner, I have an appointment to see a townhouse nearby with a room to rent.

While I'm at lunch, Arthur calls, "I need catheters! The assisted living doesn't provide them and I don't have enough!" He needs at least five or six a day to express his urine.

"Aren't you getting them delivered?" I ask.

"Yes, but they won't be here before I run out!" This is how it goes. Finding a sliver of time to fit in another errand. Squeezing in one more thing in an already busy schedule, like getting the last drop of toothpaste out when the tube is already squeezed flat.

"Can someone else go?" I ask.

"No one is available, "Arthur tells me. I'm doing the best I can, but I am getting grumpy. When I express this to Arthur, he says, "My catheters are important."

"So is knowing where I am going to live!" In the hierarchy of needs, why do mine come last?

So tired. It's exhausting to be a caretaker and find a place to live, pack, hire movers and rent a storage unit. Every day my time is frittered away. I'm not getting to bed early enough. I'm not getting enough sleep.

I resign myself to the new task of picking up and dropping off the catheters before my appointment. Then, I drive to see the townhouse. For $700, the rent includes full use of the house and my own bathroom. The owner wants a commitment of at least a year. A year is too long, too scary. I commit to six months. I explain to Kim, "My husband had a terrible accident. I sold my house and I need a temporary place to live. I can't commit to a year." Making myself human. We each have a story. This is mine.

"I may be able to work with that. I'll think about it," Kim says.

I don't know how long Arthur will be in assisted living.

I can't sit and wait for him to decide what he's going to do with his life, if or when he'll be ready to live together again. I need to take care of myself. This is a start.

Much as I like the townhome, I learned from the assisted living debacle to have another plan in place. I continue to look for other rentals. I visit another house, this one with a full basement and use of the kitchen. I'm depending on God to lead me to the right place.

When I arrive home this evening, an envelope is taped to my door. Inside, a note and a combination for a lock from our neighbor Rita, the one who came into my bedroom to collect Arthur's personal items. Odd that his storage unit is in her name.

When I ask Arthur about it, he says, "I asked her to be at the storage unit so the movers could have access. They couldn't fit everything into the current storage unit so Rita rented a small one for me." *Three storage units! How much money is that costing us?* I'm not happy but it is already done.

Then he says, "I must have done something to offend Rita. She's not talking to me."

"What would you have done?" I reply, "Maybe you didn't do anything." It could have been something I said, not Arthur. When Arthur was on drugs, trying to manage his chaos, I texted Rita and asked her not to contact Arthur about a particular situation.

"I feel like I'm in sixth grade," she responded. I feel that way too. I have to set a boundary with grown-ups who should know better than to get in the middle of my marriage. This is my life. My husband. I needed to stem the flow of crazy decision making going on.

Later, I check my emails. I am thrilled when I see one from Kim that offers me the room in the townhouse with a six-month lease. I have a place to live!!!

Then I open another one from Mom's group asking for prayers for one of our members. It isn't what I expected. It's worse. My friend has Stage Four cancer throughout her body. I am stunned. She is only in her fifties with five children.

I realize my situation could be worse. It puts things into perspective. In the gap between finding a home and my friend's dire circumstances, there is hope for me. I find a little flame of hope.

Each Day a Little Death

38

Sunday, November 08, 2015

Again, the weariness. I wake up too early, my neck throbbing, my head spinning with all to be done before settlement on November 23.

While waiting for coffee to brew, I clear two drawers. How do you empty a house? One drawer at a time.

After breakfast, I remove all of the window coverings. When I moved in, the first change I made was to take down heavy draperies in the bay window, lightening the air, the space. Now I take down the white Battenberg lace valances from the family room, the crushed fuchsia curtains in my office, the black and white curtains in my bedroom. It's like a death. The death of dreams.

I force myself to focus on the moment, only this moment, this task, because here I am okay; not emotional one way or the other.

I spend the afternoon at Becca's, enjoying chicken tortilla, watching my two grandbabies run, sing and play. Ages one and two, these children are a balm to me. Becca's home, a haven. On the ride home, I am so tired I have to tell myself, KEEP YOUR EYES OPEN.

When I get home, I badly need a nap but I see Alan's blue van in front of the house. He spent the afternoon clearing out the rest of the utility room. He's been an amazing help and he keeps showing up to finish the job. *What would I have done without his help?*

Instead of crawling in bed, my feet drag me downstairs to the teen room where Alan is, noticing the changes as I walk slowly down the six steps. Kevin's posters taken down. Games packed away. Each thing taken down, cleared out, a little death.

My dad was never in this house because he passed away two years before I moved in. Yet I felt his presence in the utility room where his tools were. Alan finished clearing that room out today. I walk in and my throat closes, my eyes well up and I begin to sob. Alan walks in, looks at me, then turns around and continues his work. He doesn't try to comfort me. Instead, he gives me the gift of allowing me my tears and my privacy.

Alan packed up several large trash bags and at least eight boxes of trash. What is in those boxes taped shut and labeled "trash"? I am not going to look in there. I couldn't tell trash from useful items among the throng of tools and paraphernalia lying around– plumbing, PVC pipes and foam. So many extension cords, paint and putty, lots of gunk of which I don't know the purpose. I let Alan do his work, trusting him to do the sorting, not having the energy or wherewithal to do it myself. I am grateful he has been able to do this daunting task.

We will have more to sort after I move, more in Arthur's storage units. I will think about that later.

For now, I push forward, worried I have so much stuff left to do; worried I'm forgetting something important – like a closet somewhere.

As much as I've tossed out, donated, given away and sold, there is so much more left. I'm sure if I culled it again, I'd find more to let go of.

But in this utility room, through my tears, I see the ghosts of my craft area, which excited me when I moved in – an organized space to put my things. I see Kevin as a teen and then as an adult building the workbench, his baseball cards stacked under the stairs. I see my dad and my grandfather in the tools left behind. I see Arthur in here too, laying claim to the utility room shortly after he moved in.

Well, it's done now, emptied. I have a headache. Too much crying. Too much thinking.

It's Too Late

39

Monday, November 9, 2015

I want to scream and yell and gnash my teeth! Sometimes the exhaustion wins, the anger oozes out, the powerlessness over this situation. I can't believe I'm moving soon.

On January 1, 2015, I had no idea my life was about to change in a drastic way.

I look forward to a new year—all the delightful possibilities! I made a list of the dreams I had this year: get my children's books published, travel to see my friend Connie, visit Paris, lose ten pounds. On January 1, it was all possible!

On June 11, 2015, the dreams were washed away. Since then, it has been a year of loss and grief. The accident, selling my home, my mom being moved two hours away, and losing my two cats, both over twenty years old. Arthur—our marriage, his broken back. Each one a painful loss, stacked like China plates, thin, fragile.

At home, I pack lamps and vases, clean out drawers, trash nails and thumb tacks from the junk drawer. Then I toss the entire organizer in the trash.

The entire porch is once again filled with donations to be picked up. Note to self: don't accumulate!

My back aches from all the bending, twisting, my shoulders tight from the strain, the muscles in my neck have been throbbing for a week. I am overwhelmed by the decisions still to be made. *How will I get all of my stuff into storage? Which belongings will I be able to bring to the townhouse?* I shouldn't have to do this alone! No one should have to do this alone. This much packing, moving and decision-making is taking a toll on me on all levels, emotional, physical, and mental.

While on the phone with Arthur, I break down, crying in the lunch room at work. I'm tired and angry at life. It spills out in anger at all the "no's" he gave me throughout our marriage. No to camping and cross-country road trips and Hawaii.

Anger that we didn't come to these decisions together. He says we did. I know we didn't, his objections overriding any discussion, any compromise. "Let's take a trip cross-country!" I said, "We could stop and visit your siblings all across the country!"

"You have to work!" he replied, "You have a business to run!"

"I could take the summer off. It's slow in the wedding business."

"We don't have the money!"

"We could rent out the house for the months that we're gone. It's the perfect time! You're retired and I work from home!"

"I'm not leaving all my belongings in a house with strangers!" And that was the end of that.

Anger at the assumptions that there was more time. It reminds me of my mom's chief complaint about my dad—he said "no" to travel when they were younger and healthier. He said they'd travel when he retired. When he retired, he got sick, and died shortly after. A good lesson for couples. Communicate. Be willing to listen. Be open to compromise. Make sure your partner feels heard. I did not feel heard. Hence the anger.

It's too late for so many things. We can't go back, but I still have to process these feelings. He apologizes repeatedly. It doesn't change the past or make it better. I dry my tears and go back to my desk, focusing on work. It helps take my mind off my problems.

Each day at home, I sort and pack and move mountains. I look around and there's more to do. Another bookcase to be emptied. Things to donate, give to my kids or put in storage.

How much fits in a 10' x 13' bedroom in a townhouse? A queen-size bed? Every little thing requires decisions, yet my life is still up in the air. Will Arthur and I ever share a bed again? Arthur is lucid, we are talking, but our future is still uncertain.

I eat late at night. Food is comfort. I need comfort. My neighbor Barbara offers that, once again. She invites me to her Thanksgiving dinner. "Hors d'oeuvres start at 3:00 p.m." *What will I do without Barbara? Can she save me again, the way she did when I moved into the house in January of 2000, depressed and missing my mom, taking me under her wing, mothering me?*

I need time, energy and space to process the feelings bubbling to the surface. I remember when my Uncle Joe moved to Florida, he sold his house in Delaware with all of its contents. Furniture, antiques, big screen TV. He packed his clothes in his car and drove to Florida. Now I can appreciate leaving everything behind and walking away.

With all the stuff I've been giving away, I might as well have done that.

Hitting My Wall Again

40

Monday, November 16, 2015

One week before settlement. I walk slowly downstairs to the teen room, the room I have been dreading, the room I left for last. It was easier to pack the linen closet, scour kitchen drawers and rummage through the laundry room. The teen room is overwhelming emotionally and physically. Before Arthur's stuff was moved to storage, it was stuffed to the gills.

What remains is most precious to me: my crafts, my artistry. My heirlooms including spaghetti bowls from my Italian grandmother. A box of memories for each child. And overwhelming decisions of what to keep and what to let go of.

As I look at the teen room, it's the picture in my mind that hurts my heart. I don't see a mess; I see a room filled with happy voices and music, beer pong and games of pool. Parties my son had…and I am choked up and sad beyond words.

Kevin hosted innumerable parties in our teen room. How many games were played on that pool table? He hosted beer-pong parties, New Year's Eve parties and a party nearly every weekend I went to Philadelphia to visit my mom. His friends crashed at our place and dropping by was so common that Kevin initiated a policy: if you've been to our house twice, knock and walk in.

Will I ever have people dropping by again? Will Arthur and I move in together again? No time to ponder about it now.

My mind floods with memories as I stand in the teen room. I see a TV and a worn black velvet sofa. Many a morning I found Kevin's friends sleeping on that sofa. Kevin enjoyed many cozy, sleepy football afternoons on that sofa too.

When Kevin moved out, the teen room languished. Arthur lined the walls with shelves for my craft supplies. He loaded shelves with containers of light bulbs, batteries. Auto supplies and boat paraphernalia. The beautiful space became cramped with chairs he never used, a TV he never hooked up, a stereo system buried under boxes of more stuff.

Standing at the bottom of the stairs, I feel the heaviness of all of this. The joys, the pain, the sadness of letting go of this space that housed many happy parties. Dreams of parties with my grandkids and passing the house along to my children that will never happen now.

I can't do it. I just can't. I don't know how I'll get this done. I don't know how to let go of this space, how to let go of my home.

I fall apart, caving. I sit on the steps, my head in my hands and I sob. There are too many obstacles, too many roadblocks, too much planning, coordinating, deciding, choosing. Too many drawers and closets and clothes left. Too much.

I can only cry in spurts, only have so many meltdowns. There's work to be done and a deadline to have it done by. I call Becca. "Can you come over?"

My angel, my Boo. She lives forty-five minutes away, has two children, a husband and a house of her own. She drops everything and drives over.

"It'll get done," she says when she arrives.

"By WHO?!!!" I reply, "Who is going to do it??? I can't! It's too much!"

She goes outside and calls her sister Ashley. She comes back and tells me Ashley is coming over. Reinforcements.

When Ashley arrives, the girls go through each box I point to: this one, that one. I am incapable of making decisions; they decide for me. "How much baking are you going to do in the next few months?" Becca asks as she looks at muffin tins and cake pans.

"I don't bake much anymore."

It's easier with someone to guide you. Occasionally, I look through things they are getting rid of. But why? I trust them. Ashley is having unexpected fun. She discovers more than she anticipated and gathers more than she thought to take home. When my girls are together, they get silly, like when they were little and I had to separate them in church because they were having a fit of the giggles. It's a gift to hear them laugh together.

After working for several hours, my girls leave, each with containers filled with craft supplies, kitchen goods or stuff to sell on eBay.

A few more days of moving, packing, tossing, clearing. Then I can breathe. Then I can dance, enjoy craft fairs, scour estate sales. I will have a life again.

Saturday, November 21, 2015 12:23 a.m.

It hits me. Lying in bed, watching an old John Wayne movie. The thing I have been dreading, worried about, just out of reach, so focused on emptying the house. But tonight, the words become feelings. Two nights left in the house. *Two.* Settlement is Monday.

It's difficult to sell a house you don't want to leave, even if it's the best decision under the circumstances. I don't know when, but these feelings will have to be unwrapped and felt. I put my feelings up on a shelf, to be taken out at a later date.

After tonight, I will have one night left in this house. I can't believe it. I want to cry. I don't want to let go. I'm not ready. It's too soon. I thought I'd have time to enjoy the house after it sold, time to sort through papers, to sit, to reminisce. Time to grieve. To say goodbye, but there wasn't time. There was always too much to do.

Why can't I have time to enjoy the last remnants of my life here?

When I call my friend Kate and ask how I am going to let go, she suggests, "Say goodbye to each room by taking in the good energy, the good memories." Gather the energy toward you, take it with you." I do this, going from room to room. Oddly enough, I feel joy. When I go on the deck, I remember the weddings, the grandkids running in the yard, the friends over for a BBQ. I take it all with me. I leave nothing but emptiness behind.

I thank the breakfast room for serving me. I see Charlie and Carolyn, Sharon and Mike and Barbara and Lee sitting on the wicker chairs at our parties. In my mind, I reach back fifteen years ago, when we just moved in and I see my family from Philadelphia surrounding my grandfather's metal-top table as we sang happy birthday to both Kevin and Ashley. And the pumpkin carvings at the table. I have photos. Good memories, fun times and photos. That's all I have left.

I don't have to leave my memories or the good energy behind. I take them with me. I am happy inside, joy-filled. *Thank you, God for all of the memories. For my wonderful life here.*

Two nights left. Will I fall apart on Monday? I don't want to face that pain. *God, help me through the pain.*

It's all happened so fast. It's all over so fast. Arthur playing ball in the yard with Ryley & Morgan. And now he can't walk. Arthur's accident in June. Selling the house in November.

So many changes, so little time. Lightning fast, yet filled with long, exhausting days.

Walking around my home my mind says, *"It's just a place, Angela."* A place, a shelter. You can find shelter and happiness elsewhere. And live an uncluttered life.

The mind plays tricks. A part of me believes when this crisis is over, I'll be back here, back to my life, back to my home. That I am on a vacation. But no, my home will be gone, on to new owners. I'll have a new life, in a new place. I try to convince myself it will feel good. But I already know it will be strange. And sad.

What's left in its place? My life is still in transition. I'm going to a temporary home. I don't know if Arthur and I will ever live together again, if we will survive this crisis or if he will ever feel well enough, strong enough to be independent again. *Will we survive this crisis, Lord?*

Long Moving Day

41

Sunday, November 22, 2015, 8:00 a.m.

I awake peacefully this morning in my home, my final day here, and go about my morning routine, making coffee one last time. Then I sit in my plush chair, set my coffee down on the wicker end table next to it and look out the bay window as I've done countless mornings before. Thanking the view, the ever-changing trees and the large window. Watching the hummingbirds feed on the porch was a gift to everyone who lived here and we enjoyed it for many years. I gave all of my bird feeders away, not knowing if I would have a place for them again.

I dreaded the final day in the house. I want to avoid this goodbye. This heart wrenching, gut-tearing final day in the home of my dreams. The home I thought would take me into the future with my grandchildren playing in the yard in the summer, splashing in the plastic pool or jumping through the sprinkler. Hosting the family Christmas Eve dinners, bringing our growing family together in the heart of the family. My home.

Can I change my mind? Is it too late? What if, what if, what if I regret it? What if I want my house back? What if Arthur and I do not reconcile. What will my life be like? It's a big empty chasm ahead.

I used to love the beginning of a school year with its fresh copybooks and sharp pencils, just waiting, waiting for me. Blank. Unwritten. A future of possibilities.

Could this be a new copybook in my life? A fresh start? I'm only fifty-seven years old. Too young to be down-sizing. Too young to give up on my dreams. But not young enough to have more of my life ahead of me than behind. My house was my retirement plan. It's all I had. Now I have nothing. I am moving forward with nothing, no home, no plan. Myself and the belongings that fit into a 10'x15' storage unit.

Kevin and Dawn arrive and stand in the foyer. My son says, "Mom, we have a little surprise for you." I feel a moment of panic, my mind racing, wondering what it could be this early in the morning on the day of moving.

As a rule, I don't like surprises. I am easily overwhelmed because I am a processer. I need time to absorb an onslaught of information.

Then he tells me. Kevin invited "the boys" over for breakfast today. My boys, whom I've known and welcomed and mothered since they were in middle school. The boys he partied with and lived with. During the previous week, I had called each of them and asked, begged for help today with the final packing and moving. Each one declined. Now I know why - they were part of the surprise.

I immediately begin crying as Tim and Rachel, Tanya and Jimmy, Charlie and my daughter Ashley, her husband Chris and the grandkids walk through the front door.

A warm egg casserole made by Dawn sits on the counter. The gang grabs paper plates and loads up, eating in the kitchen. There is no place to sit and, although it was Kevin's plan, not much time to swap stories. There is work to be done. The furniture needs to be moved out; the trucks loaded.

After eating, the gang disperses throughout the house, bringing down everything that isn't nailed down. They sweep, load the truck, and talk all at once, asking me questions.

Soon, my car is loaded, Arthur's truck is loaded. We run out of room for my mattress so Charlie ties it to the roof of his SUV.

When the house is emptied, Kevin's friends head out, leaving me to worry how I will get unpacked at the townhouse. This is the end of a long road over the past few months and I have used up my favors. Perhaps I should have hired someone to move me, but my money has to stretch. Dawn and Kevin agree to help and we head over to the townhouse in separate cars. This is not what Kevin wants to be doing on a Sunday afternoon during football season.

Kevin and Dawn arrive as well as my friends Joe and Jim, who respond to my last-minute calls, and we quickly empty both vehicles.

It doesn't take long; there isn't much– a bureau, a desk and computer, my bed and my clothes. I have to return to my house to leave it in "broom clean condition" for the new owners. Kevin and Dawn meet me there so we can say our goodbyes to the house, one last time.

I'm grateful that I don't have to do this alone. It is a sweet, poignant time. The healing goodbye I needed. I had DREADED saying goodbye to this house, dreaded leaving it, dreaded closing it up myself.

Now Kevin and I swap stories, memories. The Christmas Eve that kept growing and growing as we added one card table, then another and finally, Kevin said, "There's a door out in the trash." He took the door into the house, set it on two sawhorses, threw a table cover over it and we were ready for more guests.

We talked about all the parties he'd had here. Kevin said, "You don't know how big the parties were! People everywhere – a hundred people. The street was lined with cars." Friends of friends brought friends.

I am thankful he has such good memories of this house. The house with room for a pool table so Kevin could invite his friends over. It didn't go to waste.

I imagine the grief will hit me in pieces. Tomorrow is settlement. I won't return to the house. I've said my goodbyes.

This journey beginning with Arthur's accident five months ago, leading to this day, has been hard in every way, on every level. Emotionally, physically and mentally.

Goodbyes are final. It's their nature. You have to leave one thing behind to embrace another. Even when you're moving to something planned, something exciting, something good, you still must leave the dock to embrace the new adventure, and there may still be sadness along with excitement for the future. But I don't feel that I have anything concrete to look forward to. I'm not moving to a better situation. My future is uncertain. I expect I will be grieving this loss for a long time.

I dreaded the final moment when I would leave the house, my dream house, our family's anchor. Dawn and Kevin make the unbearable bearable and leave me with a sweet last memory. After a group hug, we walk out together.

Epilogue

July 4, 2016, 13 months after my husband's accident

I slid the key into the door and held it open for Arthur to wheel through. The hardwood floors are perfect for his wheelchair. With ten-foot ceilings and tall windows, the condo is flooded with light. That first day, Arthur sat in front of the refrigerator and asked me for a glass of water. "There's the refrigerator," I pointed, "Get it yourself." It was a first step to his independence.

Arthur told me he never thought he would live a normal life again. He thought he would be in a nursing home or assisted living the rest of his life. My goals when we moved in together were to give Arthur two things: give him back his dignity and give him back his independence.

I believe he now has both.

Arthur went back to the hospital a few more times during his stay at the assisted living. Each time he came out weak and needed time to heal. Yet at $4,000 per month, it was costing him his life savings to stay there.

Several times I broached the subject of living together. Did he want to do that? "Yes," he said, but he was afraid. I was too. In fact, I walked away many times, determined not to return, ready to be done with this relationship and the way he was treating me.

But I heard God say, "Go back. Stay with him. It will get better. It will be better than before."

What else could I do but listen to God and trust Him?

When my six-month lease was nearing its end, I asked Arthur, "Do you want to try this together?"

He said he did. I began a hunt for a wheelchair accessible apartment or condo that we could rent. This was a challenge. Many of the older places were not required to follow ADA guidelines. The doors weren't wide enough, the bathrooms not equipped for a wheelchair.

I persisted and my persistence was rewarded. I found a beautiful sunny condo, brand new. I quickly filled out the application and told Arthur. When he said he wasn't ready, my heart sunk. I couldn't afford the condo without him. Yet he insisted he wanted to do this. So, I moved in and he asked for more time. Finally, one month later, on the 4th of July, Arthur's Independence Day, he moved in.

The sunlight spills onto the wood floor of the condo as it did in my home. I sit in the mornings with my coffee and look out the window. We have a view of trees and sometimes we see deer. When I sold my house I prayed, God, if I must give up my yard, please provide a place for my grandchildren to play. God was faithful. This development has three playgrounds.

We are living a new normal. We have a comfortable routine.

In 2016, I began this book. In 2019, I left my job as an insurance agent to both care for my husband and work on this book. It has been an emotional journey and I've had to take several breaks. I had to be kind to myself, kind to Arthur.

Our road has not been an easy one. I have a lot of resentment to work through. I refuse to be mistreated or disrespected.

Today, Arthur is fully independent. He can stay alone when I travel. He cooks, sweeps, does the wash. He can shower himself and cook simple meals. Load and unload the dishwasher, do the wash. And in 2017, he got his new license to drive. We own a lime green wheelchair accessible van with hand controls, the final bit of independence.

Current day, 2021

It's been six years since the accident. It's taken me that long to process, focus on the book and finish it. I had to do it gradually because I was also trying to take care of my husband and work through my own grief. Each time I worked and re-worked a chapter, the pain was fresh. I was angry. Angry at the situation, at God, and at circumstances that played out.

Six years out, my life is better than it was before the accident. We just purchased our first home together. A one floor ground level in Annapolis, Maryland. Easy in, easy out for my husband.

God came through. He kept his promise. Before we moved in together, Arthur had an epiphany. My marriage restored; my husband more attentive. So much healing has taken place. And that is a gift. God was faithful. Our marriage is better than before.

Be on the lookout for my next book, Part II of our story, which includes our first year of living together after the accident. We didn't have a clue how to do this! Follow our journey as we work through life with Arthur as a paraplegic. If our story has encouraged or helped you, please share it with others who might need hope and inspiration - anyone in crisis, dealing with a disability or tragedy.

Did you enjoy this book? Please consider leaving a brief review on Amazon and other websites. A few sentences will help spread the message of hope and healing to others!
We'd love to share our message of hope and healing! We are available to speak to your group. Please contact us at:

theitaliangrandmama@gmail.com.

Follow our blog at theitaliangrandmama.com

RESOURCES FOR SPINAL CORD INJURIES

Below is a list of resources that are available for those with spinal cord injuries. Some my husband and I have personal experience with; others were recommended to us. I do not endorse these; I simply mention them so that you may do your own research. It's a place to start, which I would have appreciated when we were going through our journey. This is not a comprehensive list as many resources are available.

- United Spinal Association: https://unitedspinal.org/ An advocacy group for anyone living with a spinal cord injury as well as family, friends and healthcare providers.
- Christopher & Dana Reeve Foundation: https://www.christopherreeve.org/ An umbrella site that links to other resources. A plethora of information.
- Chesapeake Region Accessible Boating https://crabsailing.org/ A wonderful organization in Maryland with volunteers that offer sailing to veterans, the disabled and youth from underserved neighborhoods.
- Blue Ridge Adaptive Snow Sports https://brasski.org/about/ Offers skiing and snowboard instruction in Pennsylvania for people with disabilities.
- Move United https://www.moveunitedsport.org/ Offers wheelchair football, lacrosse, racing, tennis plus many other sports for other disabilities. A nationwide program that offers sports rehab to disabled vets, those with spinal cord injuries, visual impairments and other disabilities.

Other resources:
- Look for the Department of Disability in your county or area. Always check with your local and state government agencies. Your county government may offer valuable resources for the disabled.

- Tri-State Advocacy Project
  http://www.tristateadvocacy.com/ Advocates to help
  you process getting the help you need. They are based
  in Philadelphia, PA
- Local Boy/Girl Scout troops – they often need projects
  for badges. My husband reached out to a local troop who
  agreed to build a ramp to our front door.
- Core-Energetics https://www.coreenergetics.org/ –Not
  specifically for disabled, but this modality helped
  me release my emotions and stuck energy and was
  instrumental in keeping my sanity during the period
  following my husband's accident.
- The National Paralysis Resource Center
  https://acl.gov/programs/post-injury-support/
  paralysis-resource-center-prc

Rehabs:

We can recommend National Rehab Hospital (NRH) in WDC
through our experience.

https://www.medstarnrh.org/our-services/spinal-cord
-injury-rehabilitation-services/

Rehabs recommended by others with spinal cord injuries:

Please note: We are not familiar with these rehabs because
we have not used them, so we cannot personally recommend
them. However, they were recommended by others who have
had positive experiences. Please do your own research.

- Craig Hospital in Colorado
- TIRR Memorial Hermann in Texas
- Rehabilitation Institute of Michigan
- Kennedy Krieger in Baltimore MD
- Frazier Rehabilitation Institute in Kentucky
- Shepherd Center in Atlanta GA

And other tips:

- Sweets and sweet talk. Nurses, aides and CNA's are all your caregivers and can make or break your hospital stay. I brought them sweets (chocolates, cookies). Arthur was especially good at praising them, complimenting them on their smile or telling them how they brighten his day. A kind word and a smile can go a long way.

- Check out **Facebook groups** that are for Spinal Cord Injuries (SCI's), Paraplegia or Wheelchair Users. These are not professionals, but people living with SCI's. These have been a great resource as well as a support for us. Most are for both caregiver and those who suffered SCI's. You can ask a question or read as people share information on various topics like how to travel in a wheelchair, cathing and bowel training.

- Look for a **Loan Closet** or similar program in your area that lends used medical equipment. People donate used shower benches, wheelchairs, etc. When my husband's wheelchair broke, our development in a Senior community had a loaner shed where he was able to borrow a wheelchair for as long as he needs it.

- Check out my blog **theitaliangrandmama.com** for blogposts on paraplegia, adaptive equipment, wheelchair dancing and more. My husband and I have several YouTube videos that offer tips for paraplegics and caregivers.

Tips for rolling over a patient and using a pull sheet:
https://www.youtube.com/watch?v=qvEGyO0bcAI

Paraplegic demonstrates the use of chocks:
https://www.youtube.com/watch?v=KJN69K9HDYg

Paraplegic demonstrates how to put on and remove shoes:
https://www.youtube.com/watch?v=w7r92svK1ZM

Paraplegic demonstrates use of grabbers in daily life:
https://www.youtube.com/watch?v=dde5OWT9bls

www.ingramcontent.com/pod-product-compliance
Lightning Source LLC
LaVergne TN
LVHW051227080426
835513LV00016B/1457